UNDER THE SOUR SUN

UNDER THE SOUR SUN

Hunger through the Eyes of a Child

Elmer Hernán Rodríguez Campos

Translated by Tim Honchel

Live Solidarity Media

Publisher's Cataloguing-in-Publication Data

Rodríguez Campos, Elmer Hernán, 1969- author.
    Under the sour sun : hunger through the eyes of a
    child / Elmer Hernán Rodríguez Campos ; translated by
    Tim Honchel.
    pages cm
  LCCN 2014920665
  ISBN 978-0-9909593-1-1

    1. Rodríguez Campos, Elmer Hernán, 1969---
Childhood and youth. 2. Poor children--El Salvador--San
Salvador--Biography. 3. Children and war--El Salvador—
San Salvador--Biography. 4. San Salvador (El Salvador)--
Social conditions. 5. San Salvador (El Salvador)--
Economic conditions. I. Honchel, Tim, translator. II. Title
  HV804.R63 2015
  362.7097284'23092   QBI14-600194

Cover and interior design: Julia Navaro

Map courtesy of the United Nations. El Salvador, Map No. 3903 Rev. 3, May 2004. (p. ix)

Interior photos are provided by the author except as follows: Larry Towell / Magnum Photos (p. 14), Michel Philippot (p. 48), Octavio Duran (p. 62) Ken Hawkins / kenhawkinspictures.com (p. 71)

Published by Live Solidarity Media.

Printed in the United States of America.

Dedicated to real solidarity between people, which allows us to achieve our dreams as brothers and sisters.

— Acknowledgments —

I WOULD LIKE TO THANK the following groups and individuals (and the many more that are not listed) for their generous contributions towards the completion of this book:

Andrew Manieri, Best Semester Latin American Studies Program, Brandon Reinhardt, Greta Mackalpin, Julia Navaro, Ken Hawkins, Koinonia Farm, Larry Towell, Mauricio Perez Valverde, Michael Philippot, MJ Gentile, Octavio Duran, Patrick Hamilton, Roman Galisevych, Tim Honchel, Trevor and Laura Poag, Violet Wyum, Viria Blanco and her husband Guillermo, Wendy Honchel, and of course my family!

Bendiciones,
Elmer Hernán Rodríguez Campos

— Translator's Note —

I FIRST MET ELMER in September of 2009, when he spoke about poverty during my semester abroad program in Costa Rica. Like everyone else in the room, I was profoundly moved by his story of growing up in "the Scab" of San Salvador and his years spent scavenging for food "under the sour sun." My hope in introducing Elmer to others is that we get to know the perseverant people of non-Western nations and begin to heal the wounds that we often did not know existed in our world.

Tim Honchel
August 5, 2014

— About El Salvador —

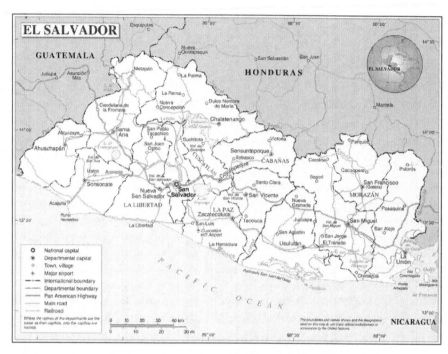

EL SALVADOR IS A COUNTRY in Central America about the size of Massachusetts. The population was 6.3 million in 2013. The income per capita was $3,720 in 2013. The primary language is Spanish. The capital city is San Salvador.[1]

1540-1820	El Salvador ruled as a Spanish colony
1821-1839	Part of Federal Republic of Central America
1840	Became independent nation
1840-1931	Governed by 14 family oligarchy[2]
1932-1979	Governed by military dictators
1979-1992	Civil War between government and guerillas

---

[1] World Bank. El Salvador. http://data.worldbank.org/country/el-salvador
[2] Owners of coffee plantations

— Introduction —

WHEN I WAS A BOY I did most things with my left hand. It felt more comfortable and more secure. For some reason, my father felt that my way of doing things would put me at a disadvantage in the world. He began to politely ask that I try using my other hand, the right hand. He argued that the world was designed for right-handed people.

Those were years of absolute ignorance and his petitions went unheard. One thing led to another, each more drastic, until one day he tied my left hand behind my back with a belt while I was eating. As a result, my movements at the table became uncomfortable and sluggish. I even remember the laughter and mocking this provoked from my older brothers. Now, many years later, my father feels ashamed for having acted in such a manner.

At that point I was three or four years old. It was a very difficult phase, like starting from scratch. When I began school however, no one would think I was born left-handed. By that time, I could do most things with both hands, except write, which I could only do with my right hand.

This would have been of no great importance, if it had not violently taught me that everything, absolutely everything could change, even our own behaviors. There is no battle fiercer or more demanding than the one which must sometimes be waged against ourselves.

Man carries a sculpture inside of him that he molds and shapes during his life journey. Based on his capacity to think, the cultural wealth he possesses, and the extent of his self-knowledge, the final result of this unique work will acquire a certain degree of consciousness and be modeled for all to see.

For me, this first battle to correct my "defect" of being left-handed was a clear warning that things would not be easy and that I should get used to situations that went against my own nature. More than anything, it helped me to conquer the challenges that arise when one is born into extreme misery, a situation that makes one feel like he is the worst of all. If he does not launch a frontal attack to that idea of despair, a person can come to believe that he was forever destined to lose.

– Elmer Hernán Rodríguez Campos

Contents

Acknowledgments vii

Translator's Note..viii

About El Salvador ix

Introduction x

1 An Ocean of Trash...1

2 Raining on Standing Water..................................15

3 The Scab 25

4 The Ugly Thing 33

5 Meetings on Main Street....................................51

6 Postcard Revelations 63

7 This is Not a Game 75

Afterword 85

About the Author..88

About the Translator 89

1

— An Ocean of Trash —

WHEN I WAS SIX years old, I lived in the community of
Soyapango, a densely populated neighborhood to the south of
San Salvador,[3] and I literally passed the days searching in an
ocean of trash. I went shirtless and shoeless, with pants that
were crusty and torn, and a stomach full of the edible filth I
found there.

But the hunger continued, stuck to the body like an
extra member, like an internal organ that had been born with
me. And that was the truth; the hunger had been born with
me, like an inheritance from my ancestors. It was my
obligation to learn to talk with her, tease her, and entertain
her while I found something to eat that was actually
worthwhile.

I had become an expert at that little game of entertaining
my stomach, which I had played since I was little. So it was
that one very memorable day of my childhood in that heap of

---

[3] San Salvador is the capital city of El Salvador. The city's population was
500,000 in 1970 and the country's population was 3.7 million. (World Bank. "El
Salvador." http://data.worldbank.org/country/el-salvador)

trash, I found something that helped me from the instant I saw it: a postcard of the snowy mountains of the United States. It served me in great ways to endure and escape from the reality of those years of incredible hunger.

During the days of intense heat, when the sun ignited in rings of fire and surged in temperature like a great fried egg in the highest part of the glass-like sky, I entertained myself by observing that postcard (I believed they were the snowy mountains of Wisconsin or Massachusetts). I told myself: in the country of the United States, life must be pleasant because if you are thirsty, you can drink snow and if you are hungry you could also eat snow. Syrup and a large bowl would solve all of my problems in that country, I thought to myself.

When the sun seemed to be against me, the stench of trash agitated me even more, and the black vultures appeared to be flying in a spiraling party over a specific point of the dump, I hurled myself down with my back comfortably against the waste, extending my hand to shade my eyes from the sun that covered my face. I was lost in the sights of the postcard and succeeded in transporting myself to happier places.

Many times, that is how I mocked the hunger and heat. Now, even though the thing is distant, I tease my hunger, talking to her, laughing in her face, and without tears I tell her "You could not beat me!" And while it's true that this is not the story of a person that began poor and ended up immensely rich, like they want us to believe a genuine success story should be; this is a sign, maybe a peek through a crack of a life like many others: a childhood shared by thousands of children born in Central America, plundered and bankrupt.[4]

---

[4] Recommended reading for historical context: *Understanding Central America* by John A. Booth and Thomas W. Walker

I was born in 1969 in San Salvador, the capital city of El Salvador. My childhood home had a roof and walls made from old tin, nailed to four rods, and buried in a dirt floor that was always muddy. My mother got up at the crack of dawn to sweep the floor, including the yard. But she could not sweep away the thick and foul-smelling scab that was born long before the dirt.

I am the last of three brothers, and to be honest, I remember spending most of the day together, roaring with laughter. One morning, when I had just turned five years old, my two brothers, Armando and Alberto, excitedly came to wake me so I would go see something they had discovered. They had been working since early in the morning to dig a hole in the yard behind our hut.

The commotion that had them so excited was at the bottom of this hole. There sprung a ceaseless blue flame, similar to the one that heats a kitchen stove.

All of the wild endeavors at that time were the inventions of Armando, the middle brother, who directed and supervised them. For some reason, my brother Armando believed he knew everything, and standing around the hole he told us with absolute certainty that the houses in the neighborhood were built above an indigenous cemetery. The blue flame sparked from the lungs of the indigenous priests. He assured us that he had heard chill-raising screams from the depths of the earth.

"Look, look!" he pointed. Sometimes the flame went out, only to return with even greater intensity. That was because the Indians were still breathing and wanted to get out and avenge themselves, my brother said, signaling to the bottom of the hole.

It's enough to say that I was the first one to go out running in search of my mother. I was terrified and afraid, but no one came out from the depths of the Earth. The one that did was my infuriated mother, who came out of the house with a broom in hand, going after my two brothers, promising to give them the beatings of their lives for having scared me and having played with fire.

Of course this was no indigenous cemetery or anything like that. The truth is that the houses in my neighborhood extended into the limits of this enormous dump. Some houses, like mine, crossed even deeper within the dump's boundaries, standing upon the wads of trash that came from the capital and some rural areas.

The flames came from the concentration of methane gas that could be found along the ground, so much so that there were sometimes small explosions. Above this time bomb we grew up with every class of disease, with epidemics that flogged us and left five to ten children dead at a time, victims of the cruel reality of poverty. Even though its name changed each time, the monster of misery kept coming to harass us. In some seasons it was the unceasing vomiting, in others it was the crazy fever, or the cruel assassin, dysentery.

Personally, I was afraid of dysentery because this epidemic had the capability of taking out an entire household. In little time, it attacked the children with uncontrollable diarrhea, absorbing their scarce liquids and engulfing their bluish brown eyes in dark shadows. Later, their strength left them until they could no longer move. They lost the battle swiftly, staying right where they were, trapped like hopeless little birds in a cage.

In that way, a child who had been playing the evening before, without the least hint of warning, became an inert and unrecognizable corpse the following day. This turned all of us into possible candidates of disease and made my mother think epidemic at the smallest sign of diarrhea. She would start to give us more liquid than usual and pray with profound faith. Here I should say something in honor of the truth, and that is that my brothers and I succeeded in leaving this stage alive, with all the odds stacked against us, due to the profound faith that my mother maintained in spite of the circumstances. The power of faith in a mother or father's prayer is not limited by social class. Even though I know some will criticize it, I believe that in itself is a colossal strength to the poor.

My mother wasn't the only worried one. All the parents who were able forbade their children from the practice of dumpster diving, the principal cause of infection and all these epidemics. Some people organized and requested a health clinic or at least the visit of a government health worker, but a neighborhood like ours is born into a precarious situation where it has no right to demand anything. The most we ever received was "either put up with the situation or leave." So around 800 families put up with the situation simply because we didn't have anywhere else to go.

The scarcity of affordable housing was problematic for a city where the majority of the people were poor[5], and many saw it necessary to move onto abandoned municipal lots. These plots, like the dump of Soyapango, were not apt for living. However, due to the impossibility of paying any kind of rent, families like ours decided to take the risk. These acts were well-organized, collaborative, and practiced frequently in those years.

In our case, the taking of land occurred when a group of men, women, and children undertook a march from different points in the city, far from the municipal dump. It was midnight and they carried all their belongings, old tin, and pitchforks to raise an improvised hut and lift the hopes of many. Above all else, they would be required to resist opposition and keep those hopes alive, even when the armed government authorities arrived to drive them out by force.

That night, April 22, 1970, I was only one year old. They say that people were shot and arrested, but the masses kept

---

[5] "During the 1970s, an estimated 90 percent of urban workers received less than the legal minimum wage. In 1977 the average daily wage in urban manufacturing and service sectors was the equivalent of US$2.80." (Haggerty, 79)

coming from all directions. As they appeared and gushed forth, the armed but now powerless soldiers were forced to retreat from the popular advance. From that moment on, in condemnation of our unjustifiable violation of municipal property, the government would deny the existence of our nameless settlement. That's how it would be, to some degree, forever.

We were denied the right to have a school, along with the right to potable water and electricity. Those last services were ultimately obtained from a power line that was illegally extended from the main road. More connections dangled from that line, illuminating all of the huts. The same happened with water; through a connection to the public water supply pipe, it was possible to bring water to every household, and public faucets had been installed in specific points of the community.

The government's response, being that it could not kick us out, was to make us put up with the trash that the dump trucks piled closer and closer to our huts. Every day, the immense heap of trash extended toward us. The compactors began to rumble early in the morning as they leveled the trash that had been unloaded by trucks during the night. Our presence tended to annoy the men that drove these machines and on more than one occasion they charged at people, without knowing that what they considered a joke could become a catastrophe.

But there was a practice that had become a way of life for the majority of the inhabitants and it was unstoppable thanks to rich people. Those who grow up rich have always had the habit of throwing away things that still have some use, above all electric appliances. These things are thrown out at the first small sign of defect and fall into the hands of the poor, who with a little patience and intelligence, repair them and return them to life. My heart would quickly throb when picking up and opening a bag to find a blender, radio, or watch and I would plead fervently to God that he would never, never take away this good habit from the rich.

This habit stirred the group of men, women, and children to turn towards the dump at the break of dawn in search of the scraps that had arrived in the night hours. It was a well-organized cycle that culminated when a merchant would pass by the houses at different hours of the day, buying the scavenged appliances at a low price in order to go and sell them at a good price downtown after a quick fix-up.

The business was straightforward for him. His name was *Don*[6] Octavio and he was a giant, dark-skinned man, poorly spoken and smelling of sweat, without an expression of kindness on his face. He would never let a coin slide to help his neighbor. On the contrary, he turned all of these virtues upside down to demonstrate to others that he had left being poor behind. He therefore felt contempt for the people that had not attained the same success he now showed off. And so that no one would doubt his success, he wore long gold chains around his neck, gilded rings on his dark fingers, and from time to time he would take out his wallet full of money, as inflated and fat as his belly, and hold it for all to see.

He drove a red Chevrolet truck that would appear at any hour of the day, through the same dusty street entrance as the trash-filled dump trucks. Everyone used to feel overwhelmed with happiness in his presence, some for having brought things to sell, others to buy new things. We kids, in general merriment, would follow the journey of *Don* Octavio in his red Chevrolet running in the middle of a smoke-like cloud of irritating fine dust. Even in the wet season when the dust became impassable mud, the truck's arrival caused a wide-ranging cheerfulness.

The story of *Don* Octavio, as it is told by none other than my know-it-all brother Armando, was that at one time he was the poorest man in the entire world, but that life had brought

---

[6] *Don* is a formal Spanish honorific reserved for men of high esteem

him to this heap of trash where he became a millionaire. Some adults also reinforced my brother Armando's version of the story and said that *Don* Octavio once searched among the trash like all of us. He searched in the morning, afternoon, and night, until a night came when he could do so no more and he submitted to a deep sleep in the midst of the rotten heap. In his dream, he saw a man dressed elegantly in gold, with gold-pointed shoes, a golden watch, chains, rings, and even golden teeth. The "gentleman dressed in all gold" said to *Don* Octavio that they would make a pact; *Don* Octavio would give the gentleman his soul and the elegant man would reveal the location where he had hidden a wooden box replete with bars of gold. When he came to this point of the story my brother Armando would open his eyes wide and try to make his voice terrorizing, the children would look at him expectant and alert, and then he would continue.

In this profound dream, *Don* Octavio delivered his soul and the man dressed in gold took him by the hand to the agreed upon site. When he awoke, he could not believe it; his head was reclined above a wooden box like the one he had just seen in the dream! Upon opening it he found a thousand bars of gold, one laid comfortably on top of another, enough to take him out of his poverty.

Whether it was a deal with the devil or not, we kids swore and promised one another that when we were older we would be like that, like *Don* Octavio, the most successful man to ever walk the face of the earth. It was in pursuit of that dream of leaving poverty that some of us would go into the deepest part of *la Costra*[7], the name I remember the place by, hoping to someday find a wooden box with bars of pure gold, like the one *Don* Octavio found that day.

This indescribable possibility sustained the people every day: that if *Don* Octavio had found a box of gold it was because there was another box or two awaiting the next

---

[7] Spanish for "the Scab"

millionaire. No one knew how to explain this thesis, but every time that someone came upon something similar to a box, all nearby activity stopped.

My brother Alberto experienced it once when he opened a cardboard box that some thought was empty, but held a wooden box inside. The silence of those of us who were close by was swift and I believe that everyone's breathing thickened and grinded, like the needle of an old record player beginning to streak across a record. I looked into the face of my brother Alberto and he was a breath away from bursting into tears. My brother Armando, who already felt rich, had begun to prance strangely, followed by a dance of celebration.

"We're rich! We're rich!" they said while we hopped about the Scab on one foot. But it wasn't bars of gold that were inside, it was an old television, heavy like they made them before they invented the Formica frame. People must have seen the cardboard box before, but no one had imagined that what was inside was a television; above all one in such good condition that when we arrived home and plugged it in, the device began without trouble and worked in a normal manner.

We entered into a world that we had never seen before. All I can say is that this brought a lot of happiness to our childhood years and reaffirmed to us that the world and all it had to offer was worth the trouble. More than happiness, that box of dreams introduced me to my first love.

We had it for perhaps nine years, and every evening after coming home from school, I would sit between the other kids to watch the series *"Blanco y Negro,"*[8] that was about two orphans who were adopted by *Señor*[9] Dromons, a millionaire that brought them to live in his penthouse. This series was shown in the 70's and was very well liked among the children

---

[8] "Diff'rent Strokes" was a television show that ran from 1978 to 1986 about a rich Manhattan family that adopted the children of their late African-American maid.

[9] *Señor* is a Spanish honorific meaning "Mr."

in my neighborhood. Watching the television, my brother Armando would say, "What great luck those dark-skinned kids have!" and it gave us hope that *Señor* Dromons would someday appear and decide to adopt us.

I wasn't betting on that, and so I dreamed that life would place Kimberly Dromons, the only daughter of the millionaire bachelor, as my imaginary sister. I believed that if I loved this blonde girl, born in the flavorful country of edible snowy mountains, I was capable of defending her love with hard punches to any boy that would dare to say that she was his girlfriend. In fact, many times I returned home with bruises on my elbows and a bloody nose because I fought off their fists in defense of that "love," perhaps the most tormenting and, it surprises me to say, the first virtual love registered in modern history.

The actress that played this person was named Dana Plato, and this cool lady that also experienced serious problems in her life[10] left this world without knowing that in Central America there was a boy dying of hunger that wanted her crazily and loved her electronically, and when I say crazily I don't lie, as the other boys considered me a great lunatic. Misery permits this kind of fantasy free of charge. Like some dreams, these kinds of childish fantasies dissolve over time like soap bubbles in the air, until they remain forgotten in complete anonymity.

Since I was a boy, I've had many of the same dreams of other kids my age, dreams that desired to be someday fulfilled. I saw myself crossing frontiers and arriving in countries with names as remote and fantastic as Norway, Iceland, or Morocco. I dreamed of visiting cities, the names of which I saw in the pages of a dictionary in our house. I sat at tables replete with food as pleasing as the names of the cities themselves. I wasn't the only one and I accept that, but

---

[10] Plato, an American actress, died in 1999 at age 34 after overdosing on painkillers. She struggled with substance abuse and unemployment for many years.

everyone decides whether or not to write their story and this one is mine, located in one of the poorest and most unpleasant countries of the world, governed mostly by military assassins that serve absolutely no purpose but the mass murder of people.[11] In the massacre of 1932, the dreams and lives of 30,000 *campesinos*[12] ended in the midst of their heroic insurrection[13]. The military leaders demand to be called "Most Excellent President of the Republic." All this they heave upon the dignity of the people they have terrorized.

In the midst of this fear and ignorance, our grandfathers and our fathers were formed. And so they raised us, denying us what was forever denied to them, not daring to lift their heads and see the sun every once in a while, to stand among the rich face to face. The poor man had been made only to serve the rich, without protesting, without daring to emit a single sound, without even dreaming that someday a rich man might pay attention to the words that a poor man might say, if he might someday dare to say anything at all.

As one acquires a certain degree of conscience, he realizes that some acts aren't personal. Rather it is the unconscious collective of ignorance that passes through time. That's how I came to understand my father's alcoholism. That vice was not his alone, because for most of our fathers in those hopeless years, the alcohol represented an upward bound exit that would make them forget their suffering. But the more they got to know the drink, the more misery it would produce.

---

[11] El Salvador was ruled by a 14 family oligarchy from 1838 to 1931 and military dictatorships from 1932 until the start of the civil war in 1979

[12] Spanish for "peasants" or "farmers"

[13] After the military overthrew the oligarchy in 1931, the indigenous peasants rebelled in 1932. The attack failed and for several years, anyone wearing distinctly indigenous dress was targeted by the Salvadoran military. This military action became known as *la matanza* ("the killing") and estimated peasant deaths were 15,000 to 30,000. (Haggerty, 16)

In my family, the majority of times were bad times and if there were moments of any abundance it was by the luck of bumping into something of value in the dump, our second home. From time to time, someone would throw out a scream of happiness and raise their hands in a sign of victory, for they had managed to see some golden chain, or watch, or something that could be sold to calm the hunger in the house.

This was not a common occurrence, but it did happen. And as life sometimes does itself justice, one good day, bright and beautiful from the moment I awoke, it was my turn. I was seated, looking at my postcard of the snowy mountains of Massachusetts or Wisconsin, using the reed of bamboo in my hand to strike a random and insignificant bag. I was dreaming that I was in the photo; sliding on my belly along the white mantel that covered the mountains. I opened my mouth as wide as I could to swallow as much snow as possible as I traveled down at high speed.

Just thinking about this extinguished the extensive heat. My hand, on its own accord, continued beating the broken bag with the bamboo reed until a pair of pants appeared among the waste. They felt heavy, like there was something inside. I guarded my postcard transporter and looked through the pockets of the pants one by one, my fingers shaking as I opened the front pockets. Nothing. Then I tried the back pocket. Nothing. Then the other: *¡Santo Cristo!* There it was in all its splendor: a medallion with the virgin Mary attached to a thick chain, interlaced with three large-sized graduation rings.

I remained silent, never having seen something like this, not even on *Don* Octavio, the only one who wore that kind of jewelry. I went to my brother Armando and we found our other brother, Alberto, to go home together. My mother was overflowing with genuine happiness. The next day we went downtown and my mom sold everything at a good price to a friend with a business in the municipal market.

It was one of the grandest days of my childhood. I felt important and tall in stature, which was partly due to the tennis shoes my mother bought me as a prize for my luck. There was also enough to buy a pair of pants for my brother Armando and a watch for Alberto. My mother also took advantage of the moment and bought a piece of fabric, which my father used to make her a Christmas dress. I can still remember it; it was blue with yellow flowers and she looked beautiful in it. Next she bought back the sewing machine that she'd been forced to pawn off months earlier, motivated by our great hunger. We returned home with everything, and cherishing the recovered sewing machine, my father promised all of us that our turn to be happy had now arrived.

We all believed him for a long time, but his alcohol problem was stronger than his wishes, and in little time we were already back in the same situation or worse, because a dream had faded away.

My old man was a good person and a magnificent tailor. That skill was the result of a home broken by the early death of his mother, who passed away when my father was nine or ten years old. From that moment on, his upbringing, and the upbringing of his seven siblings, was in the hands of his father, another tailor, who under the excuse of being a widower, delivered himself to alcohol.

The scarce scholasticism of my father taught him nothing more than to read and write, but he was a very capable person and can still strike up a fluid conversation about any subject with anybody. When he succeeded in abandoning the drink, my father dedicated himself to us and to the tailoring workshop that consisted of a sewing machine, needles, thread, enormous scissors, a ruler, and a table where he cut the fabric. That table was also where we ate. He was and is a fine tailor, and clients visited him from other neighborhoods on the recommendations of other clients.

My father liked to teach his vocation free of charge. He recruited young people to teach them the secrets of tailoring.

Some succeeded in perfecting the trade and years later dedicated themselves to sustaining their families with that practice. When "teacher Carlos" was sober, everyday was a *fiesta*[14]. I still remember him with a colorful ribbon around his collar, a pencil in his ear, giving instructions to some apprentice about how to stick a button or to make the edge of a pant sleeve. In those seasons we didn't have to look around in the trash because my father's work fed us.

However, those periods came and went, and on any given day he might appear reeling down the liquor next to other drinking colleagues. Everything went under and the story started over. The hunger that had been hidden off to a side of our intestines sprung up again, and so began the long seasons under the sour sun.

Municipal Dump of Soyapango
1991 photograph of the dump where Elmer grew up
and scavenged for food.

---

[14] Spanish for "party"

2

— Raining on Standing Water —

TWO OR THREE DAYS before it arrived, the news informed us of the hurricane's advance and its devastating destruction. Its center was located in Honduras, but it was so strong that it extended into the neighboring countries of El Salvador and Nicaragua. The radio said to store food, potable water, and have a first aid kit with basic medications in reach. They also warned of the risk of staying in vulnerable low places and flatlands.

We the poor didn't pay any attention because that whole message was not for us. How were we going to store food? If and when we had any food, we consumed it immediately. The same concept applied for water. As for the risk of staying in vulnerable places, perhaps our houses faced a greater risk of danger, but where were we going to go? We simply had no other option but to stay there, waiting to see what would happen. That was the reality for the vast majority of people.[15]

---

[15] By 1983, approximately 75% of San Salvador's inhabitants lived in slums. (Haggerty, 79)

At that time, I was five years old; it was the month of September 1974 and I remember very well what happened. The first drops fell in the early morning, accompanied by a lot of wind. We three brothers slept squeezed together in the same bed and I was not the only one to notice that the storm had arrived.

When the day dawned, the drops had already become a persistent rain that fell about the rackety roofs and trickled down into small currents through the dusty road, which was now the color of dark chocolate. Above the garbage dump's steep and extensive mass arose a thick and pestilent cloud.

We children were happy because, due to the emergency, the public school was closed. We asked our parents for permission to swim in the rain. That first day in which we were supposed to have been frightened, we, the children of our neighborhood, considered to be a national *fiesta*.

The rush and screams of children getting soaked in the rain masked the sound of the wind whirling between the tall branches of the trees. Some branches were knocked off into the puddles and the children used whatever piece of wood they could find to build small surfboards. They threw themselves on, lying on their bellies, swimming down the street.

A large pool had formed in a ditch, and my brother Armando was trying to impress a group of young ladies his own age by launching himself from a large stone in reckless dives to the water below. Not quite dives, they were more like clownish belly flops. The water kept falling and we all pleaded to God that the amusement would never end.

The water did not stop falling. The night arrived and it continued raining with greater strength and the wind flogged the little houses like old boats tied to a rickety dock. The following day, we again returned to enjoy the amusement that nature was giving us, but seeing the fury of the wind and noticing that the water was turning black, we realized it wasn't much fun anymore. The annoying and unstoppable Hurricane Fifi had arrived, soaking everything in its path.

By the third day of the storm, there were reports of missing people in some parts of the country. The rivers were overflowing, flooding crops and villages, and important bridges were collapsing in the fury. The hurricane itself stretched 400 kilometers[16] from its center in the coast of Honduras, where it completely destroyed the town of Choluma and took several thousand victims.

In my neighborhood, the poorly constructed shacks had fallen down. Even the roofs and walls of the huts that remained standing were somersaulting away in the wind, allowing wind and water to pour in from all sides. My house became so damp that in a single moment, I couldn't tell whether it was wetter inside or outside.

In response, my father placed our most valuable belongings on top of the table in the dining room. The meager inventory could be reduced to a television, an iron, and a battery-powered radio. He threw a big roll of plastic over all those things, and it stretched from the table to the floor on all four sides, forming a tent-like structure inside the house. That's where we placed our only mattress and stayed for all those days.

I felt perfect in that place. It was the only spot that was warm and dry in that entire deluge. My family made room for me in the middle and I fell asleep listening to the sound of the raging wind, counting the drops one by one as they fell from the numerous leaks in the roof into the tin cans we placed below. In the midst of all those sounds, like a murmur in my ear, I heard the unending prayers of my mother.

I remember Hurricane Fifi for the wet muggy days and the deafening thunder that woke us all one early morning at dawn. We got up and discovered that a thick municipal wall

---

[16] About 250 miles

had fallen down on at least five huts, flattening all of their occupants.

In my neighborhood, that was the saddest part of that emergency. Two of my friends were found among the wreckage, along with four friends of my mother, and two troublemaking companions of my brother Armando.

A few days later the rain began to let up. It came and went, weaker each time until the sun finally returned to dry everything out. It was incredible that houses like mine remained standing, but they too wanted to stay alive.

Little by little, life returned to normal. In a matter of days it was as if nothing had happened and the activity in the garbage dump started anew. That's where we spent most of the day, as school had been closed for 22 days while they repaired a classroom damaged by a fallen avocado tree.

That's where we were one evening when my brother Alberto went running toward the main road. "*Tio*[17] David! *Tio* David! Here comes *Tio* David!" He yelled excitedly and ran to meet our *Tio* David, who had returned after spending two years in the region close to the border with Guatemala. He had worked there in whatever job presented itself, and he came to see us, worried in case something had happened to us during the hurricane. He brought us presents, some money for my mother, and a new hat and gilded rivets for my father.

Tio David was a lifelong fighter. His great desire to overcome adversity drove him to learn on his own what others could only learn through academics. He knew how to take blood pressure and inject medications. Based on his daily reading, he diagnosed illnesses and prescribed natural medicines that he mixed himself, so accurately that it was only a matter of hours before people's ailments improved. He didn't dare to charge for his services because he wasn't a doctor, but he did tell his patients that if they improved with

---

[17] Spanish for "uncle"

his prescription, they could give him a voluntary contribution.

He lived from those contributions and was fairly well off. People came looking for him at our house in the morning, in the evening, and sometimes in the night. But he had one big problem: *Tío* David had learned to cure others but he never found the right plant to cure himself of a severe and chronic asthma that had plagued him since childhood.

When these attacks arrived without warning, *Tío* David didn't have the strength to get up out of the corner where he slept. My mother made us give him the only bed with a mattress, where we slept, and there he crumpled himself up in a small mountain to pass his asthmatic crisis.

It was sad to see him in that state. He would open his mouth as if he wanted all the oxygen in the world to enter into his withered lungs. The veins in his neck would inflate and turn blue from exertion. Likewise, with each cough he seemed to let go of a portion of life. The worst of it all was that no medication had any effect on him. After long years of suffering, his asthma had weakened his immune system and as a secondary effect he was not able to have children. So it was *Tío* David's fate to walk the road of life alone, accompanied only by his asthma.

Nevertheless, *Tío* David practiced elevated habits of hygiene. Even though he had only one shirt and pair of pants, he washed these garments every day and asked my father to lend him the iron so that he could remove the wrinkles and folds. Likewise, he bathed, shaved, and trimmed his fingernails every single day.

My brother Armando, the know-it-all, invented the story that *Tío* David had studied in the United States. He worked there until he became a millionaire, but he was here because he liked being poor more than being rich. My brother claimed that people paid for *Tío* David's consultations at a price that he, or perhaps my brother, had already established.

He told this story without my *Tio* David's permission, but as nothing remains hidden between heaven and Earth, one fine day my uncle discovered my brother's tall tale and Armando was punished.

Our lives changed drastically when *Tio* David came to live with us. I liked that he was there and tried to behave well. It was almost always me that he took along on his outings, when he had to give someone an injection. For those occasions, I bathed, put on clean clothes, combed my rebellious hair, and hit the road at his side. I was immensely proud of having David as an uncle.

People bid us to come in and I began to watch all his movements intently. First, he would check the patient and take the temperature of their forehead with the backside of his hand. Then, with his always-clean fingers, he would gently open the patient's eyes and light up their pupils with a small lamp, looking thoroughly for several seconds. He would take their blood pressure with equipment that he had obtained from who knows where and write some numbers in a small notebook. At the end, he would take out his injection case which was full of glass syringes and needles that he sterilized for each new patient.

When treating with injections, he would only do so if a certified doctor authorized it. In other words, people contracted him to do nothing more than administer the injection. Apart from that, no one noted that there was any difference between my *Tio* David and a certified doctor. When we returned home in the evening, he would always buy me a soft drink and cookie from the store, in recognition of my good behavior.

It didn't please him that children were walking about the dump. He tried to get the parents to comprehend that it wasn't healthy, but he was unable to convince everyone. In order to entertain us with something else, he built a chalkboard and had us do addition, subtraction, and some multiplication tables. It was thanks to these assignments at home that I learned to read and write well before I entered school. My mother and father were eternally grateful.

Sometimes when we were watching television, the news anchors would report something, and when the journalist stopped talking *Tio* David would ask us what our opinions were. After listening to us, he explained what he thought and gave us facts that made his opinion extremely interesting. The same thing happened when he read the newspapers. No longer conforming to the way things were or accepting how the media presented them, I would go to school and talk with kids whose parents had never talked to them about these subjects. In the worst of cases, their parents supported the positions of the government, which were of course always false.

One time *Tio* David brought a newspaper clipping with a photo of some men in the mountains. Everyone was clothed in faded military attire, with long hair and beards. He pointed out one of those men and said, "This here is a great leader; when he gives an order, he doesn't say 'you go,' he says 'let's go.' With men like Fidel Castro, El Salvador would not be like this." That was the first time I heard that name.

Of course, this way of thinking brought my *Tio* David problems. In those years, the media presented Fidel Castro as an assassin of children, so a declared admirer could be compared to a criminal terrorist. *Tio* David soon lost respect and the majority of people began to distrust him.

This led my *Tio* David to not stay long in the same place. For that same reason, one day, about three months after his return, he once again took up his satchel with his books, magazines, and the medical instruments that saved lives. He went away in his only outfit: a pair of brown corduroy pants and a long-sleeved white shirt.

I had to climb the branch of a mango tree behind my house to watch him fade into the distance. There he went along the main road, carrying his incurable asthma on another uncertain course. There went the one who was responsible for my first learning of letters and numbers, for my appetite to read everything, and for my Christian principles on this Earth. He used to say that Earth was where those principles proved to be most valuable. There again went *Tío* David, forever the lonely migrant.

Tío David
Photo from David's personal ID

It existed before
That intrigued asthmatic child
Who asked questions
Waiting for someone
Anyone even
Who could give an answer
To all that he had seen

But his stunned reptilian voice
Was lost in the city walls
Submerged in its wonders

Time trekked down the road
With the unstoppable urgency
Of that which will always be forgotten

At its pass, the trees burst out
In flowering fruits of concrete

And the boy
Is now a silent wall
His questions unanswered

3

— The Scab —

DURING MY EARLY YEARS, poverty was no more than a word that adults used to somehow explain why things didn't turn out well in life. Some people used that word to justify their alcoholism. In other cases it was used to justify idleness or poor hygiene. These people blamed poverty for their shortcomings, saying, "Life has punished me with being poor and therefore I drink. I don't look for work because I'm so poor that I can't do anything. Taking a bath every day is for rich people."

And that's what a person grows up to believe, until he realizes that's not how things are. In my personal case, until I was five or six years old, the word poverty did not worry me in the least. I was happy because I didn't know how far the limits of my poverty reached.

I spent the greater part of the day laughing at everything or nothing. Every minute, even with hunger, seemed interesting to me. I felt lucky to have an immense garbage dump at my disposal and I considered the children who lived far away from it to be less fortunate than me. Besides, I had gigantic mango trees all around me, and I could climb them whenever I wanted. In the end, poverty arrived only when an adult mentioned it.

This happened around the time I entered school. The school was attended by children from other communities that were far from the dump. These children were poor too, but their parents had told them that they were rich and that they should humiliate those of us who lived in the municipal dump and look on us with disdain.

There are parents that believe they can conquer their poverty by telling their kids they aren't poor, but when those children go out into the street and face the real world, they come away with a delusion that is twice as traumatic.

Like I said before, it all coincided with my entry into the scholastic world. The children from those other communities seemed to enjoy reminding us where we lived. When they saw my brothers and I with friends from our neighborhood, they generally greeted us by saying, "Ugh! The scab has arrived," or they would say, "Here come the kids dying of hunger." I did not know that such an insult was a mortal offense, so I could not understand why my brother Armando and our friends would run over and fight them.

My brother Armando would give the sign of attack. He would answer them, "Yeah we're hungry, but we've got some knuckle sandwiches for you!" Finishing his last word, he would plunge into the expansive group of opponents, growling to instill fear, and throwing kicks and punches like a crazy man. The others merely imitated him.

So it was that a circuit in my brain was suddenly activated and I asked myself, "Why are we poor?" I discovered that this question had already been asked by the majority of children my age. They were also asking, "Why do we have to look for our food in the dump? Why do we have to live off of what others throw away?" And that's when the question "why?" started to carve its way into my days and nights. Things seemed to be no good anymore and I discovered that the word poverty weighs more than one hundred planets combined.

At that point one starts to torment his parents with questions like, "Why are we like this? Why are other people not like this? Why don't those who have a lot give us half so that we can be equal? Why? Why? Why?" And our parents didn't know what to tell us because their parents had also not known what to tell them. It came to the point where we questioned them so much that we put them in a bad mood.

Sometimes I thought it was forbidden to ask for food because it brought the adults so much despair. The best example I can remember is when my mother, in the midst of scarcity and tribulation, exclaimed "Who the heck would invent the idea of three square meals? As if it's not difficult enough to eat once a day!" Our minds were nurtured by all those experiences and sometimes I thought that eating was not a basic necessity but rather a bad habit.

Time passed and we came to the conclusion that hunger and its resulting condition of inferiority is neither an outdated concept nor a red current transmitted covertly by communists in other countries[18]. No, hunger is real and I know it because I spent my entire childhood hungry. I went to school, played, and slept, always hungry. I ate filth from the dump and was always hungry. I learned to do the same as my brothers and friends and fight the kids that humiliated us, and whether I was giving punches or receiving them, there was hunger, governing our lives and pushing us into problems.

That kind of hunger leaves a man with lifelong scars and he must fight hard to forge a better path for the future. Many roads will present themselves, some more uncertain than others, and only one will be right for us. We will arrive at that road if we have the necessary tools.

---

[18] Authorities often blamed civil unrest as the work of foreign communists from Nicaragua, Cuba, or the Soviet Union

When I say tools, I'm talking about education, because it's one thing to be an educated poor person and it's another thing entirely to be an uneducated poor person. When I say education, I'm not referring to a poor person's elegant language or manners, but to his academic education. A poor person has to study even though it is harder for him than it is for the rich person. There is no alternative, because learning is the tool needed to evade those short-sighted options that are presented to the poor person sooner or later in life: vices, gangs, prostitution, etc.

It's true that having a profession would be ideal, but it's also true that in most cases this is impossible. So we begin with the first priority, a desire to read and learn everything we can. With that, the poor person is off to a good start to face the ups and downs of life and he can make it so that the only difference between him and the rich person is money. I talk about money as if it were nothing because knowledge, action, and feeling weigh more than money in the balance of life.

No one can deny that in the last 30 years or so, school has arrived in places where our grandparents could never have imagined. Before, it was more difficult to learn the basics of reading and writing. Now, if a person doesn't know how to do even that much, it is due to a complete lack of responsibility for himself and his children. The most valuable inheritance a parent can leave his children is the desire to learn and exceed, to be better every single day.

For the most part, every child desires to become someone in life, to change his situation if it is tormenting him. I say this because around Christmas at the end of every year, volunteer groups came to visit children in extreme poverty. With their cameras and microphones ready, they would throw out the same old question as always, "What do you want to be when you grow up?" We were all very familiar with that question and not one of us ever answered, "I want to continue being poor." No. All of us, absolutely all of us, aimed to fly as high as our dreams allowed and we answered, "I want to be a doctor," or ""I want to be an engineer," or "I want to be president," or "I want to learn everything!"

My brother Armando, who was the most troublesome of the bunch, and who always felt the need to say something funny, typically answered, "I'm not going to be any of those things. I'm going to be a millionaire." His reply died beneath the sound of the visitors' laughter.

The part about becoming a millionaire, my brother Armando has not yet fulfilled, but as for not becoming an engineer, doctor, or president, he was successful. He presently has his sights set on becoming an anthropologist, and with the same pointed stubbornness he had as a child, he's almost made it.

These groups would give us a cookie and a soft drink and then leave, carrying our voices and dirt-filled faces away with them in their cassettes and rolls of film. Surely at least one of those photos they took is walking around here or there. Maybe someone has published it to illustrate some graphic about the poor children of Latin America. Or maybe none of them exist anymore, I don't know. In any case, I was the dark-skinned boy with big ears, scrambled hair, dirt on his face, and no shirt; the one that's laughing in front of the camera in every single photo, alongside two magnificent brothers and a group of beloved friends, some who are now dead from the war or from hunger.

The point is that a poor person has to conquer his poverty and not let the word "scab" make him lose his way on a journey that is very difficult from the start. The poor person must fight to conquer real poverty, not the lies handed down to him. Living in poverty is made even more difficult when one swallows the message designed to make him chase material things. For the most part, these things are not vital, but the poor person is told that if he does not have them, he is even less than a miserable wretch. Since the time he was born, he has been told that he is and will always be a Mr.

Nobody. That registers in a poor person's brain and stays there until he sure enough feels like a miserable wretch if he does not acquire these material things that the great merchants assure us no one can live without.

If the poor person someday succeeds in getting most of these things, it is believed that he is no longer poor and he starts to feel that he is rich. A car, television, or gold ring does not mean that someone is rich, but the message is "Get things, even if you don't need them, and you will look like a rich person."

And so the poor person, descended from other poor people, runs after these things, leaving the real fight with poverty on the side, the fight against ignorance and more specifically the culture of poverty. This culture of poverty is cruel because it is full of complexities, frustration, and feelings of insignificance. A person can live without a car, the latest cell phone, or three televisions, but someone who does not know who they are, where they belong, or where they come from is destined only to lose.

When the poor person acquires certain knowledge about his historic reality, his past, and the past of his ancestors, he stops worrying about the trivial things like the millions of dollars that he doesn't have and that his family never had. He discovers that before pursuing material wealth, he should first pursue the cultural wealth that is indispensable and in some ways free.

A small amount of reasoning ability and knowledge of self is enough to make a person never condemn himself for being poor. He will not accept mediocrity or the idea that he is and will always be poor. Having a real understanding of his situation, he will maximize the tools he has to confront his historic poverty.

Children in Elmer's community
Photo given to Elmer by a visiting organization in 1978

Elmer – front row, far right
Alberto – back row, far left
Armando – back row, second from left

— The Ugly Thing —

IN A CONVERSATION that took place before he left, *Tio* David said, "The thing is becoming ugly." Night had fallen and my parents were talking with him in the corner of the house where we had the kitchen. *Tio* David took small sips of steaming hot coffee and every once in a while would blow into the cup to cool it.

We children had gone to bed, but I had not yet fallen asleep, and I watched them through a small hole in my covers. They all seemed to be very worried.

"The people are arming themselves and there are villages in rural areas that the guerrillas call 'liberated.' There, the guerillas are the government."[19]

"Are you saying the war is becoming serious?" my father asked, deep in thought.

---

[19] Left-wing guerilla organizations such as the FPL, ERP, and PRT led uprisings against the Salvadoran government starting in the mid 1970's. In 1980, they formed a coalition known as the Farabundo Marti National Liberation Front, or the FMLN

"You must take care of the children, and above all Alberto, as he's almost of recruitment age."[20]

"My God!" said my mother, "But he's a child."

"They don't care; the Guard has no compassion," warned my *Tío* David. "If anyone resists, they kill him right there on the spot. I'm not lying, this has happened several times."

"God protect him!" my mother finished saying, and very alarmed, she returned to the gas stove with a fork to turn over the plantain chips she was frying in a pan.

It was true; the thing was ugly. Not long before, four bombs had exploded downtown after some university students had stolen the necessary equipment from a faculty member. The National Guard arrived, and whoever they did not kill they captured and "disappeared." In the end, this was another form of death.[21]

At that time, I was eight years old and in second grade at school. Among the teachers, the word "subversive" had become fashionable. That word, which I had not known before, was their way of naming urban guerrillas.

When something really important happened, the average journalist would say this word and everyone would repeat it as if they wanted you to understand that the peace had ended and it was that word's fault. In a way, to say "subversive" was to more or less mention the devil. Not only that, they recommended that every honest and decent citizen detest and combat that word, because otherwise the war would go to Satan.

---

[20] The median age of the Armed Forces of El Salvador, FAES, during the Salvadoran Civil War was 15.8 years. 46.7% of soldiers under 18 joined voluntarily. (Beth Verhey. "The Demobilization and Reintegration of Child Soldiers: El Salvador Case Study."
http://siteresources.worldbank.org/INTCPR/882274-1111741856717/20626759/elsalvadorcasefinalwannex.pdf)
[21] Guerilla activity intensified in 1977 amid reports of increased human rights violations by government forces and death squads

Truthfully, I was not very worried at that time whether the subversives existed or not. In fact, I felt a certain sympathy for them, because even though no one had told me, I knew that these people were like me. In some way they represented my condition of hunger, but as I was still very little, they neither disturbed me nor led me to dream.

I still carried the postcard with the snowy mountains of the United States and with it I succeeded in escaping my distressed reality. I would just plop myself down anywhere and dream to appease my thirst and hunger.

I will never grow tired of declaring that life always brings justice. One day something new and good began to arrive at the immense dump, by the ton. The large food companies, whether due to overproduction or simple strategy I don't know, threw away entire portions of expired food in a "noble gesture" towards us, and we enjoyed it in all of the houses.

Personally, I had thought that food chooses a person. I could not believe that someone in the world could choose what they were going to eat or not eat. For a long period of time, sardines chose me. A company had thrown away their corroded and expired cans and that food became a perpetual part of my childhood menu. My mother was given the luxury of serving each person an entire can at every meal.

"We're eating like rich people," my brother Armando would say, his mouth and cheeks wet with sauce.

"These are times of abundance," my father would say.

"This is what it means to eat well," my brother Alberto would say.

"Know this. God doesn't forget the poor," my mother decided, and we turned to our rations in silence, grateful for such a delicious delicacy.

The boxes of expired sardines continued arriving each day by the dozen and there we were to carry them to our tables. Everything seemed to be going very well, as if a rosy path had appeared before us.

But, my God! When the weeks went by and you had to eat sardines for breakfast and sardines for lunch and sardines for dinner, it didn't taste very good anymore, and every meal became a real punishment.

So it was that a marvelous idea occurred to my brother Alberto. Of the three children, Alberto was the one who thought most sensibly and when the family passed through difficult moments, he was the one to discover the solutions to the problems. He designed a plan that consisted of altering the date of expiration on each of the cans and giving them a general touch up before going off with my brother Armando to trade the product in faraway places.

At the beginning they did very well and came back from those expeditions with money or different things to eat. But like my grandmother would say, "As soon as a poor person appears to be well-off, he will be put back in his place." The customers began to complain about the bad taste of the sardines, ending my brothers' intentions of becoming businessmen and the possibility of eating anything other than the blessed cans of expired sardines.

Those were long months that we endured, but just as we had to get used to the things that went against our own nature, we also had to keep living in the inferior conditions that the Scab provided. We carried inside us the sad reality that to the government and outside world, we did not exist. We lacked many things, among them a public school, but our parents knew that we should study, so they sent us to a school in the closest community, about four kilometers away.[22]

The community was called *Buena Vista*[23] and the school also carried that name. There was only a schoolyard, six classrooms, and teachers that had no supplies. The principal was Mrs. Alma Muñoz, but in our neighborhood we called her *Alma Negra*[24], due to the rough way she treated us. She

---

[22] About 2.4 miles
[23] Spanish for "good view"
[24] Spanish for "black soul"

definitely did not want us in her school. To her and a certain group of students, we children that lived in the outskirts of the dump were simply "the scabby ones". We didn't have anything and we didn't deserve anything either. As I mentioned earlier, this whole situation put us in open war every day, and those of us who were "dying of hunger" always left losing.

According to *Alma Negra*, life had rewarded her with no children and she lacked nothing, but among her favorite students, the one she declared to love like a son was Arturo Lara, the school bully and son of a commander in the National Guard.

You didn't have to look very long at this boy or stop looking at him very long. For either of those two things he would start up a fight with you. He would always win, given that he was bigger and better fed than everyone else. Once out of mere boredom he made me eat a knuckle sandwich.

He was always surrounded by a group of friends that celebrated everything he did. That time he gave me the knuckle sandwich, he also threw me on the ground and kicked me until I became flour on the floor. His group of admirers broke out in laughter. I went to get my brother Armando, and Arturo gave him a sound beating too. The group of followers continued laughing out loud. Armando and I went to fetch our brother Alberto. The beating was doubly great for him. Then to finish his work, he gave each of us a kick in the spine. The three of us were left sprawled out in the schoolyard.

Alma Negra did not pay attention to any of this, as she and Arturo's father were very good friends. One day, by charge of this commander, Principal *Alma Negra* decided to hold a census. The intent was to verify the names and ages of those that were close to turning fifteen years old. Obviously, those of us who were below that age did not participate in the census. It was done in the principal's office and every child had to pass through and declare their exact date of birth.

Even though he was around that age, they didn't have Arturo participate in the census.

In groups outside of the office, we all speculated what this might be about. Some thought they were going to form another school. The biggest dreamers, like my brother Armando, contended that they were going to bring presents for Christmas and wanted to know which children did not need them. According to him, it would be those who were about fifteen years old, given that at that age, they didn't need toys, but to work. That was my brother Armando's version. I wanted that version to be the true one and I began to dream of beautifully colored soccer balls and toy cars.

When the census was over, *Alma Negra* sprayed the entire office with air freshener. She made a disgraceful gesture and walked immediately to where the commander stood with the list of names and birthdates of those who were about fifteen years old, the ones who according to my brother Armando, they would not be bringing presents to for Christmas.

That was early in the morning, before class, and I passed the rest of the day dreaming of the toy they were going to give me, but nothing happened. Neither did anything happen in the following days and the whole thing was forgotten, at least for the moment.

I studied until second grade in that school, which was all the schooling I ever had as a child. In those two years, I perfected my handwriting, which was already rather advanced thanks to the classes I received at home from *Tío* David. It was not until much later, in another country when I was much older, that I finished my elementary education in a school for adults, but in El Salvador, second grade was as far as I made it in terms of academic education. Some had to make due with that level of education for the rest of their lives.

One of my best friends from those years was Miguel, who we called *Chelito*[25], because his skin was very white; at least a lot whiter than the rest of ours. We were very good friends and always hung out together. We also stood up together to Arturo Lara, the bully, and he left us laid out and without air on the schoolyard floor, the favored stage for his whims.

Chelito lived in the same neighborhood as me and his house was about twenty houses up from mine. Like me, he scavenged the trash, but it was in school where we became real friends. He had no mother and lived only with his father, who worked as a cook in a bakery that paid him very poorly. Even so, *Chelito* had no need to look for his food in the dump, and if he did, it was simply out of habit.

He was two years older than me and a sure marksman with the slingshot. Where he put his eye, he put the stone. *Chelito* was very considerate of me, and when his well-aimed slingshot succeeded in knocking down a ripe mango, which was appetizing to everyone, he would take out his knife, cut it in equal halves, and give half to me. He did the same with the loaves of bread that his father brought him from the bakery.

Sometimes he would carry a bag full of breadcrumbs and share it with all his allies at recess. Those banquets came to an end when Arturo, the commander's son, suddenly came and took the bag of bread from us, to step on it or throw it in a puddle.

This happened again one day during first recess. For Arturo, who could not be stopped by anyone, it was not enough to take away the bread; he also picked up the trampled breadcrumbs and rubbed them in *Chelito*'s face. Arturo's group of allies laughed more than ever.

Chelito didn't do anything at first. He just watched Arturo fixedly while he cleaned the rest of the bread off his face. Arturo and his friends, satisfied about what they had done, began to walk away. They used their elbows to open a path for themselves among the multitude of curious people who

---

[25] Spanish for "milky"

had gathered to watch the bully's most recent act of "grace." The admirers' laughter resounded with profound echoes in *Chelito*'s ears.

What happened next was like a movie or dream. I saw *Chelito* reach his hand into the back pocket of his pants, take out the slingshot, and begin the procedure he undertook every time he wanted to score a perfect hit. It consisted of stretching and separating each rubber thread. He loaded the best stone he had found, stretched the sling the as far as he possibly could, and paused his breathing. He aimed with great calculation, closed one of his eyes a little, and released.

No one on the face of the earth could have had better marksmanship. All of my desires for destruction (and those of the majority of children in the school) were fulfilled in that perfect hit. The projectile was a direct hit to Arturo's head and even though it seems cruel on my part, I felt a great exhilaration upon seeing the one who was believed to be invincible cry; to see him there, rolling about in pain, in a condition similar to that in which he left all of his victims. Without a doubt, it was a great gift that we all thought was from God Himself.

What happened next was clearly tremendous. Professor *Alma Negra* came running in to find out what the problem was, and she could not control her fury. She took it upon herself to hit *Chelito* on the head with a broom, screaming like a maniac, "Savage! Savage!" He defended himself using his hands, but the hits were so strong and continuous that several succeeded in reaching their target.

When she tired of striking him, *Alma Negra* ordered some professors to detain him and tie him up so that he would not escape while she went to the military command post in search of the commander. He would not be pleased to see his favorite son bleeding from the head, and even less pleased to know that the one who had caused it was nothing less than a scab. We weren't able to say anything; we still couldn't shake our amazement.

We were left even more amazed when we saw *Chelito* slip away from the two professors that were holding him. In an open race he made it to the tall iron gate and cleared it with a single leap. That was the last time he was seen in school.

Three days later, when everything had returned to its relative calm, Arturo, now sporting a bandage on his head, was already running about the schoolyard oppressing whichever soul bumped into him. That morning, when we were all in our classrooms, the recess bell rang several minutes earlier than usual. We were called to the schoolyard and arranged by grade. The commander had arrived, accompanied by at least six pairs of National Guardsmen. This was the first time this had ever happened at the school. It was not caused by the slingshot incident, but it did coincide. Professor *Alma Negra* said in brief words that those who were called should step forward and form a group apart from the rest. She began to read a list of names.

"Ricardo Villatoro, to the front. Ernesto Garcia, to the front."

There was complete silence; the environment weighed on us like a dark cloak of absolute uncertainty. Every one of the boys they called left the group and with great fear situated himself among the other group that was forming. Everyone they called had been one of the fourteen to fifteen-year-olds recorded in the census several days before.

"Miguel Molina. Juan de Dios Carranza. Francisco Navas..."

Alma Negra continued reading at least twelve more names. When she finished, she fanned her face with the sheets of paper from the list to alleviate the suffocating heat and signal the end of the activity. Next they ordered us to return to our classrooms. They loaded the boys whose names had been called into a military truck. We never saw them again.

That day's lesson was on civil duty. It was explained to us that at a certain age, every citizen has the obligation of serving the "fatherland", but that sometimes the fatherland decided to take citizens at an early age to instruct them in the labors of sovereign defense. This was one of those "sometimes," made necessary by the threat of subversive terrorists that came from Cuba to cultivate the death of the Salvadoran fatherland.

In charge of this discussion was Principal *Alma Negra* herself, and she went from classroom to classroom to be sure that we all heard it.

"In other words, children," she said, "What you have just witnessed is a recruitment that the fatherland, by means of its distinguished National Guard, found necessary to perform in order to guarantee order in our country."

I didn't understand any of this, but I did think about those boys they had just taken away. Some of them had been paralyzed with uncertainty. At least three of them left crying inconsolably because everything indicated that nothing good would come of this. I knew all of them very well, as most lived in my same neighborhood. We had played together since we were very little and searched like *Don* Octavio for hidden treasures in the dump. We all knew of our shared reality of poverty and limitations.

My thoughts ran back through my years with each one of the boys, until I stopped on Francisco Navas, who was a very good friend of my brother Alberto. He was fifteen years old and very intelligent. "Paco" Navas was small for his age, but I always saw him as mature and having all the answers. He had spent almost all his life living off the leftovers of the rich. Paco Navas had a ranch seven times the size of my house and lived there with his grandmother, who was completely blind. They were an inseparable team, grandmother and grandson, walking through the dusty streets of the dry season. They were accompanied by an invisible steel bond as they walked hand-in-hand, blind grandmother and sharp-sighted grandson, down the paved boulevards of rich peoples' residences. Those well-swept sidewalks were very familiar with the footsteps of Paco Navas and his grandmother.

"Excuse me, *señora*[26], could you spare a coin for my grandmother?"

"Don't bother me, bum! Find a job, scab!"

"Thank you."

I pictured Paco Navas and his blind grandmother eating together from the food people had given them. She ate a larger portion, as he had more strength to endure hunger. Paco Navas, given to his grandmother only two hours after he was born. Paco Navas, whose mother "China" Navas had left for Guatemala because it was one step closer on her journey to the United States, never to be heard from again. Paco Navas, learning to shake off the jabs and punches of life.

Paco Navas, recruited by force into the National Guard, obligated to defend a cause that was not his but that of the rich people who humiliated him. Paco Navas, seated in the military pickup truck, scared to death and hiding his tears so as to not infuriate the guards that recruited him even more. Paco Navas, clenching his lips, swallowing the sorrows that danced in his throat as he thought of his blind grandmother, the woman who had raised him. Paco Navas, above all thinking and crying that he did not want to be a soldier.

But of all of these things that happened, at least for my family, it was daily hunger that tormented us the most. There was a serious period when the food we wanted never arrived. My brother Alberto had entered adolescence and wanted to eat everything that was put in his path.

His build was normally thin, but during this period, his body asked for double portions of food. When it didn't get the food, his system protested with frequent sickness, strange infections, and alarming weight loss. Eating expired products for most of one's life robs the body of its will to fight and leaves it vulnerable to all kinds of illness. That must be why

---

[26] Spanish honorific for "Mrs."

Alberto's nose would begin to bleed uncontrollably, his stomach would ache mightily, or his lips would turn blue for no apparent reason. No one knew how to explain it. The health system in El Salvador simply did not exist for us.

I remember how every morning during this time, after my mother woke up, her motherly instincts would carry her towards us. From one moment to the next, all the attention, and any good food that came in the house was for him. Armando and I were very understanding and never had a problem with it. We didn't want him to die, something that all the prognostics ensured would happen sooner or later.

But for Alberto, the crisis passed and he became one more survivor of the cruel war that has forever flogged the countries of Central America without mercy: HUNGER. I write it in capital letters because its denunciation has to be that big.

Like I said before, we were born with hunger. It may have hid camouflaged among our internal organs. It may have chewed our intestines with more fury at some times than others, but it was always there. I went to bed thinking about eating. My dreams were full of delicious and exquisite food. I dreamed of rice and meat with salsa, soup, and dessert. Just imagining spaghetti took my breath away, but I would wake up and reality returned with empty plates. The hunger settled in my organs and in my blood, rising like a powerful vice.

Someone might say, "Why don't these people work to mitigate their hunger?" And that was the root of the problem: there wasn't any work.[27] The general situation of the country was terrible. The farmers emigrated from the country to the city in search of work and those that lived in the city stuffed the entrances of the factories in search of work applications. The answer was that there were no vacant positions. The

---

[27] From 1978 to 1985, the unemployment rate rose to 33% and the number of private jobs decreased by 17%. Most who were employed earned below minimum wage. (Haggerty, 107)

government officials, tremendously corrupt at all times, laundered funds to family and friends. My father left every morning in search of work and returned in the evening even more disillusioned. Sometimes he succeeded in getting a little food, carrying it home without difficulty.

No one wanted to eat expired sardines anymore, because daily consumption eventually produced a severe intestinal infection that had already killed several children. Protests stirred in all the neighborhoods and everyone was ready for war. It was for this reason, HUNGER, that war began in El Salvador. I'm not just talking about hunger, but also the resulting conditions that caused great suffering among Salvadorans. For me, the hunger was made even crueler, because it coincided with the government's historic unleashing of massive repression. This repression was designed to intimidate, but it actually made many people more conscious of their situation and struggle. This consciousness is the most powerful weapon that people can acquire.

Sometimes a major event is needed for the majority of people to become conscious of their situation. A fatal or traumatic event almost always makes this happen. Even though I was ten years old, with all ten years spent in extreme poverty, enduring hardships and limitations, I wasn't interested in knowing to which social class I belonged or should support. Then something truly disturbing happened and it affected me greatly.

Chelito had not come back to class for three or four weeks. As he was a good friend of mine, I was used to going home and looking for him so that we could play or rummage through the dump. Sometimes when I got out of class, I found him waiting for me at the exit, slightly hidden so as not to be seen by Arturo Lara, who had sworn to avenge himself at all cost.

It was no secret to *Chelito* that Arturo's father went looking for him on various occasions. According to *Chelito*, a patrol had been sent by the commander to watch his house and had not moved from there all night. At least five times, *Chelito* had to hide and sleep in the branches of a tall mango tree. Because of all this, *Chelito* was never at peace and wherever we were, he was nervous. Every short while, he turned again to look in all directions. At one point he expressed that he had repented from having shot that stone at Arturo's head, even though we knew that *Chelito* was in the right.

Even with the weight of his alert state, he was sometimes able to disconnect himself from the situation and his spirit grew more relaxed. It was then that he succeeded to win every object he bet on in the game of dice.

In those days, the collectible cards from the TV show *Chavo del Ocho*[28] had hit the market. The cards could be colored in and we children were dying to fill them all in. So when we had a duplicate card, we traded it for one we didn't have. When a card was valuable, it was played for with dice, with whoever lost paying twenty cards. *Chelito* was not only right on the mark with the slingshot, he was right on the mark with the dice and every game of chance that poverty could invent. He always had the card that other people lacked. So among his beloved legacy was a thick roll of cards, accumulated by luck with dice.

One day, he had a better streak than usual and began to win and win. All the forces of good were with him that day. The group's excitement did not allow anyone to unglue their eyes from the rolling of *Chelito's* good luck dice.

Suddenly, a voice could be heard. "Finally, I've caught you, evil scab!" said the commander of the National Guard.

The entire group scattered. Some ran off in such a hurry that they could not be seen through the dust kicked up by their fleeing feet. I also ran, but the bond of close friendship

---

[28] Mexican show ran from 1972-1992 and told the story of an orphan named Chavo in a poor neighborhood

steered me to stop after a few meters and hide behind a stone.

From there I could see the commander grab *Chelito* by the hair, while another kicked him square in the stomach. *Chelito* couldn't do anything; he simply closed his eyes and tightened his lips harder with each strike. Sometimes, he put out his hands to protect himself, but it was useless. The poorly fed, poorly lived boy could not get away from the uniformed soldier, who now decided to bend *Chelito's* arm behind his back, reducing him to helplessness. I wanted to scream and call for help, but there was no one, absolutely no one present to intercede for *Chelito*. It is curious, how at times things lend themselves for the devil to carry out his plans.

They dragged him to the car, which was parked a few meters back, and threw him like a package into the rear trunk. Only after they left did I abandon my hiding place and return home, muted by all the images I had just seen.

That was the second to last time that I saw *Chelito*. The last was two mornings later, when I came to feel that everything was a pointless, complete mess. I was awakened by my two brothers to see something that the whole neighborhood was already observing.

"Poor boy; they left him unrecognizable," my brother Armando said during the walk. A large number of curious people amassed at one site in the immense dump. Some ladies were crying while they spoke nearly silent prayers with swift moving mouths. A space opened so we could see. Little by little, I swallowed in one of the sourest tastes I experienced in my childhood.

There he was, torn like trash, beaten and bloody, like I had hoped to never see him. There he was with his mouth sealed by dry blood, with one eye more open than the other, as if in his agony he had wanted to take one more look at this ungrateful world that was always rough with him; one last look at this world of social chasms and divides, a world that erases the smiles of some people forever.

The forensic judge who collected *Chelito's* body found his most prized possessions in his pant pockets: an almost erased photograph of his mother's face, a stone-throwing slingshot, a laminated medallion of the virgin of Guadalupe, and a thick roll of colored cards.

National Guard of El Salvador
National Guardsmen arresting members of popular political organizations

The start was equally sad
The city of our birth was never the same
It discovered its true face
And interlaced between its asphalt walls
Our still fresh screams

So began the night
Persecuted by uniformed bats
Our first night
Shoulder to shoulder with future death
And the present dead

Why city at war?
Why did you decide to be a sure blow
A stone above our childhood of glass?
You gave us no time
To choose our belongings

The storm was excessive, angry
And marked us forever
With the prompt condition of goodbye

Now, we are not dead
Nor do we live
We travel over the ashes
Of the broken distant voices
We emerge from the dust unburied
To inhabit the shadows between

5

— Meetings on Main Street —

FROM THEN ON, death decided to reside among us. I had seen
death before; in fact I once saw two drunk men kill each
other with machetes. I still remember how, in the roar of
combat, they stabbed at each other's body, head, or wherever
the ignorant edge of hate would fall. Suddenly, one advanced
and the other retreated. Then the other swung the machete
strategically and the one who had advanced now retreated.
All of this occurred in the midst of their children's screams
and their wives' cries. Afterwards, it was traumatic to see the
two men thrown lifelessly to the ground.

On one occasion, I also saw the corpses of three children
who died from the dysentery epidemic that scourged our
settlement at various times of the year. One of those children
lived next door and played with me on numerous occasions.

But *Chelito*'s death did make me comprehend, in all of its
magnitude, the dimensions of life and death. After seeing his
cadaver in the dump that morning, where they had thrown
out his body like any old piece of trash, I didn't speak again
the rest of the day. I went to my bed and didn't get back up.

When my older brothers came to invite me to play or to tell me something that had happened in the daily comings and goings of life, I turned my back to them and didn't pay them any attention. My mother told them, "Leave the boy alone. He's very sad, but it will pass."

My sadness did not go away. The days passed; a week went by and even though I sometimes got out of bed, I ate very little and I appeared to be getting very sick. I was disenchanted with life and continued to see it as a complete mess.

One time, my brother Alberto took me with him to buy candy at a nearby store and before we arrived, we ran into *Don* Miguel, *Chelito*'s father. The poor baker appeared to have aged forty years in little time. The death of his only son had affected him greatly and he now wandered about, talking to himself through the neighborhood streets. He didn't work anymore and instead roamed through the avenues, dreamlike and crazy, asking whoever was there, even the stones, if they had seen his son. His son, according to his confused mind, had not returned since the night before. But a month had already passed and he had not succeeded in digesting the death, so much so that in the evenings when night was coming, *Don* Miguel could be heard screaming in the streets with a crazed voice: "Miguel! *Miguelito*, it's getting dark and it's time to go to bed, son!" He would say this, then abruptly enter into a crisis of uncontrollable crying.

"To him, *Chelito* is still alive," my brother Alberto told me. I identified with the state in which this poor man found himself. He didn't know it, but we both suffered for the same person: he for his beloved son, and I for the incomparable friend. Then I knew that I was not alone, that he and I suffered because we missed *Chelito*, as many in the neighborhood missed him.

While he was alive, *Chelito* had been the cheerful soul behind all the games created by children in my neighborhood. Therefore, there was no troublemaking without *Chelito*. For that reason, whenever it occurred to someone to play something and he wasn't there, we all agreed that we should first go fetch *Chelito*. We would find him at his house doing his assigned chores. In a house of just men, *Chelito* would be sweeping the broom along the dirt floor, wetting it with a few drops of water so it wouldn't sweep up dust. He would be washing the scarce kitchen utensils or starting the oven fire to make hot coffee when his father would return.

When *Don* Miguel brought home the leftover bread from the bakery where he worked, *Chelito* would give everyone a double ration and would carry a large bag so that we could all eat on the way to our next adventure. So it was that his death affected all of us, but it was more evident to me because for some unknown reason, he decided to call me his best friend. This was inexplicable given that he, a skilled ballplayer, lucky gamesman, and magnificent slingshot, had no reason to walk alongside a sluggish ballplayer like me. But in the end, relationships are like that: mysterious. One side almost always helps the other, depending on the circumstances.

Like I said, I was unable to forget that tragedy as the days passed, but little by little I began to recover. The country's situation remained difficult. Disfigured dead bodies appeared every day in the streets. There was already talk of a popular guerrilla army in the mountains and a better-organized militia in the city. In the rural areas, the National Guard and the army massacred humble farmers without compassion, their only crime being that they were poor. It was as if being poor was the fault of low paid laborers. They united in unions and protested in popular marches, but ended up extinguished by the shrapnel of shame.

By 1980, the streets of San Salvador were boiling with popular discontent.[29] The protests had massive support and the government's response to this support was oppression. So it was that there were daily deaths, and in the dump during my childhood, another type of waste began to appear with more frequency: corpses. Bodies mutilated by the cruelest torture, done in the quarters of the National Guard. The majority were unionists, communal directors, or student organizers of marches and protest activities.

The first corpse that appeared in the dump was *Chelito*'s and it was a tragic incident by its nature. But to tell the truth, as the country's situation got worse, the appearance of dead bodies became more frequent, to the point where it became routine to come across them.[30] And when I say routine, I am not lying when I say that a person can get used to seeing dead people, because during this time period I saw many, and the later ones, although it sounds cruel, no longer surprised me.

One time we went with my father and mother to the town of Verapaz[31] in the department of San Vicente and I saw thirty dead bodies together. The night before, paramilitary forces had entered the town and took people out of their beds as they pleased. The town remembered that night as the darkest night in history. The troops arrived and after knocking down the door, they took out all the men and carried them into the street, where they either laid them on

---

[29] In 1977, General Carlos Humberto Romero won the presidential election with the help of blatant election fraud and voter intimidation. Fearing insurrection, a military junta known as the JRG launched a coup in 1979 and attempted some land reform to placate the masses, but wealthy citizens and the military prevented the measures from taking place, leading to further protests.

[30] An estimated 35,000 Salvadorans were killed by death squads from 1980-1983. (Arnson, Cynthia J. "Window on the Past: A Declassified History of Death Squads in El Salvador" in *Death Squads in Global Perspective: Murder with Deniability*, Campbell and Brenner, eds, 88)

[31] Located 35 miles to the east of San Salvador

the sidewalk or shot them point blank with one bullet to the face, right in the sight of their wives, mothers, and children.

When my parents and I arrived the next day, the assassinated bodies were still on the sidewalk in front of their respective homes. Some were side by side, some were mouth to mouth, on top of others, but all of them assassinated without even the smallest hint of compassion. Among the dead were my father's brothers, *Tio* Tono and Andrés, and Andresito, Andrés' 11-year-old son. Andresito had wanted to prevent the assassination of his father and for that he was also shot. Even though this act touched me directly, it didn't throw me off balance. I knew that I had already endured a lot with respect to war and death.

My father had quit drinking by then and even though we all thought this tragedy would be the detonator for him to start the vice anew, that wasn't how it worked out. This time he had learned to manage his emotions better. The immense sadness from the loss of three close family members served to reaffirm for him that it was worthwhile to keep fighting for life and those that we love. That's why he sewed and manufactured clothing during the day and sought a second job as a night guard. Perhaps having two activities that were in some way profitable helped him and this time he quit drinking for good.

For her part, my mother also sought a job and became a servant to a rich family in *Colonia Escalon*[32]. The woman my mother worked for had been poor prior to marrying a millionaire, and perhaps for that reason was good with the employees. Sometimes she paid my mom more than the established wage and almost always let her take home the food left over from the day.

---

[32] Spanish for "doorstep colony," smallest of the 6 districts of San Salvador, and one of the wealthiest

That was without a doubt the only good time we had, and every Saturday, there was money to buy ham *tamales*[33] for breakfast from a woman who sold them on the main boulevard. I ate two *tamales* accompanied by black coffee. My brother Armando, who was always hoping to do the most far-fetched things, after swallowing his five *tamales* ration with gluttony, then began to pummel the leaves with salt in order to chew them like a pig. Based on his theory, the leaves gave him a lot of energy, like Popeye's spinach. My mother lost her peace with him for that, but it was fresh food that tasted rich and didn't have to be taken out of the trash. It tasted so delicious to us that my brother Armando had no trouble finishing everything.

The sardines were history and the light of hope seemed to shine everywhere. From that point on, even the sun didn't seem to bother me and it was no longer like an immense fried egg cracked over my head. Everything, even the dump, seemed to have a pleasant odor.

On Sunday mornings, my dad tuned the transistor radio to the mass from the metropolitan cathedral. The voice of the man that spoke, a voice inerasable in my memory, referred to the poor and the injustices that were committed against them. He mentioned the neighborhoods of Soyapango, talked about the slums that surrounded the immense trash dump, and I felt like that voice was talking about me, my brothers, my parents, my uncles, my neighbors, and even the deceased *Chelito*. I felt like that voice emanated from a person that lived with us, knew of our search for food in the dump, and knew of the epidemics and hunger. In the end, a clear voice with all the characteristics of our language asked the rich people, in the name of God, to have more consideration for the worker and farmer, and for the National Guard and army to cease the repression. This whole message attracted us

---

[33] Traditional Mesoamerican dish of corn dough steamed or boiled in a leaf wrap. The leaf is typically discarded.

greatly and there is no Salvadoran in this age who could not identify with this Sunday message that came to us from the metropolitan cathedral, in the voice of this pastor who I had the good fortune to meet on one occasion in person. It happened like this:

The first meeting was on *Don* Paco's back porch. They gave a glass of *horchata*[34] and a piece of quesadilla to us kids. A man arrived with a guitar and sang songs that spoke of the poor, the right we had to live with dignity, and the need to organize. *Don* Paco, the host, had led the taking of land years earlier in order to build that slum. Among others were those who had solved the water and light problem that I wrote about earlier, and for that reason were greatly respected by the people. When all was finalized, they told us that for the next activity, we needed to invite the greatest number of people that we could. So on Saturday evenings, our neighborhood began to be visited by people from outside, who came from unions, universities, and above all the progressive Catholic Church. The people attended in numbers because the leaders possessed what every politician desired to have: the truth. They talked about the things that tormented us most, like hunger, for example, or how to offset the effects of cruel epidemics.

After many Saturdays, when the meetings were no longer meetings but massive rallies that took place on Main Street, it was announced that there would be a mass the next Saturday with a leader from the Catholic Church. No one knew who would be coming to visit us and we speculated the whole week over what person would dare to come and share life with the poor, and above all bring us the message of Christ through mass in the dead center of the dump, of the Scab.

---

[34] Traditional beverage which in El Salvador typically consists of morro seeds, rice, cocoa, cinnamon, nutmeg, sugar, and vanilla

Saturday arrived and early in the morning my mother made the necessary preparations to have a general bathing room at our house. We attended that evening event, well-bathed and clean-clothed. The organizers of the activity seemed nervous and would have given all they had to ensure that the National Guard did not appear that day. If they did, everything would go south, but by good fortune that didn't happen. The oppressive National Guard never arrived and everything went as it was hoped. People gathered in groups around a makeshift stage. Suddenly, a blue Volkswagen microbus appeared and we all ran to meet it. When it stopped, I stood among the front of the mountain of anxious people waiting for that person to come out and see who it was that everyone had been talking about. The sliding doors opened and he came out. There he was with his black robe, tall frame, gray hair, Salvadoran nose, and ample smile.

There he was, about two feet from my face, the man who from the metropolitan cathedral pulpit defended the poor people like me, my friends, and my brothers. Yes, there was *Monseñor* Oscar Arnulfo Romero y Galdámez, martyr pastor of the Salvadoran people[35]. The people crowded around; they wanted to see him and pushed those of us in the front. He stretched his hand high to greet us and that's when he saw me in front of him. His clean, scabless hand came upon my head in a friendly fashion, lightly turning my hair, which my mother had combed with a lot of Vaseline for the occasion. It lasted seven or eight seconds. Behind his big, thick glasses, I saw him and he saw me.

I allowed myself to be joyful for that moment. I was a deathly hungry child at that time, with only one pair of pants and two shirts that I wore only occasionally so as not to waste them. That detail seemed significant to me and if there is anything that motivated me to write these notes and

---

[35] Archbishop of San Salvador from 1977-1980. His canonization as a Catholic saint was pending as of this book's publication in January 2015.

entries, it is above all that Saturday evening of 1979, in which this martyr pastor touched my head with his hand. I would soon be ten years old, and that moment served to make me feel important, reaffirming for me that life cannot always be completely rough. I say this because it was comforting to know that people from the outside, people that did not live within the slums of Soyapango, people that were on the radio and television, came to live among us, demonstrating their filial obligation for and with the poor and hungry.

This priest's visit led many to participate more actively in the popular movement. So it was that in one moment to the next, our grassroots group became more engaged in the grand marches that took place downtown. The movement was already underway and there was no going back. The people in the meetings assumed more commitment each time and now talked to us about military dictators, revolutionary militias of the people, and so on. They would call the rich "oligarchies" and with this new language, even though we stood in the back due to our young age, we started to become new people. This type of movement gained wide acceptance through the surging hearts of the people, and in short time reached great dimensions. The assassin government's response was massive repression.

There were thousands of deaths in that time; boys and girls, men and women, captured in the streets on their way home from work and cruelly tortured until they were dead and unrecognizable. Like I said before, that's how a new type of waste began to appear in the municipal dumps, like the one where I lived close to twelve years of my childhood.

It was inevitable; the liberation message gained more strength each day and those in the "other faction" designed whatever counterinsurgent strategy occurred to them. They began to visit our neighborhood, the one they had always forgotten among all the government's plans, with greater frequency. One day, the mayor of Soyapango arrived, accompanied as usual by soldiers, and offered tee-shirts for the formation of youth soccer teams. It excited us children at least, and I remember that my brother Armando and I enlisted our respective teams without hesitation. For some time, he was the stellar goalkeeper of Carioca and I was the ambidextrous striker of the Aguilas Soccer Club.[36]

But there was a serious problem: none of us had soccer cleats and we had to play barefoot. And as the majority of us did not cut our toenails more than periodically, the balls popped or we were injured every once in a while. Buying cleats for each one of us was not among the mayor's "benevolent" plans and the thing ended after some time without the slightest effect.

Sometimes, mainly on Sunday evenings, people from the mayor's office arrived in military trucks. They passed out bags of wheat and cans of vegetable oil and powdered milk in a campaign that in those years was called the Alliance for Progress[37]. People turned out in large numbers and the lines for food sometimes extended a quarter mile below the sour sun.

My mother brought me with her to collect the parcel of food. In each bag came a small can of vegetable oil, one pound of wheat, and two pounds of milk, which managed to evaporate in spite of the protective bag. It changed into a hard block that had to be pulverized with a hammer to make it edible. Its flavor was a bit salty with a light taste of codfish, but I liked it and sometimes I broke off a generous piece with a knife and went about eating it like it was candy. When we came back from receiving food, the young face of my mother, the face of a healthy and beautiful indigenous woman, radiated with great happiness.

"The *gringos*[38] send us all of this so that we don't die from hunger," she would say.

---

36 Names of popular soccer teams in Brazil and Mexico, respectively

37 Formed by US President John F. Kennedy to foster economic cooperation between the US and Latin America

"And if the *gringos* send us flour and wheat and oil, do you think sometime they can send us a little bit of snow?" I asked her.

"Oh my, son! That's impossible," she answered, laughing humorously at my funny remarks.

I was ten years old then and believed that it was possible for the Americans, the *gringos,* to share their snow to mitigate the thirst and hunger of all the children in the whole wide world. I thought if they didn't do it, it was because the *gringos* had something against me.

I still kept the old postcard of the snowy mountains of Wisconsin or Massachusetts and just by looking at it my obsession grew even more. All of the children had their obsession and mine was the postcard. It ended forever in a violent turn of events around that time

---

[38] Spanish slang for English-speakers, especially Americans

Archbishop Romero
Archbishop Oscar Arnulfo Romero greeting a group of Salvadoran children

6

— Postcard Revelations —

IT ACCOMPANIED ME for at least the first seven years of my childhood. I found it inside a bag that also contained used notebooks and loose pages of old magazines. Surely someone had received it for Christmas or it was a memento from a trip to those lands, I don't know. The truth is that it didn't seem like much to anyone, but to me it was a great incalculable treasure and thanks to the postcard I succeeded in evading the scarcity that I lived through each day. I never had pretty toys, but I didn't need them. Everyone used to guard the memory of their favorite childhood toy and mine, for no reason at all, was that old postcard.

During those years, I protected it from the cold, the heat, and the dirt; and in those days of Hurricane Fifi, when the water rose into the house, I slept with it so it would not get wet, beneath the plastic that served as a tent during the emergency. It was mine and the designer, without knowing me, had made it for me. They made it to tease and trick the ancestral hunger that governed me. It was for my exclusive use.

The postcard was something that worked only for me. I know this very well because I once revealed its magic power to my brother Armando and he looked at it fixedly, without moving his eyes, and after a short while came back to me angry, saying, "Liar! Liar! This doesn't take away hunger or thirst. What it does more than anything is give me a headache!" He left in search of something more fun. Then I knew that everyone had their personal trick to escape reality and my trick was the postcard. It ended forever one evening, when I was playing soccer with my friends and brothers.

It was a summer day and the sky was painted with beautiful colors. A strident sound began to rumble from the south side of the sky. As it neared, the sound grew louder and louder, shaking the houses' old tin roofs. Flying very low, almost directly above us, appeared the first, second, third, fourth, and so on. One after the other they arrived until there were twelve. Twelve modern adaptations of prehistoric insects soaring through the sky.

My brother Armando, the know-it-all, signaled at the swarm with his dirty finger, spat to one side, dried off the sweat on his forehead, and spoke with certainty, the kind of certainty with which he always spoke even though he knew absolutely nothing about the subject.

"Those are military helicopters, and with only a push of a button, they shoot thousands of bullets that in a single second turn us into butter."

My brother Armando was definitely right this time. The military troops' boots were sticking out both sides of the helicopters and on the underside, on the belly of those devices, were the large letters: USA.[39]

---

[39] The US provided $4 billion of military and economic aid to the government of El Salvador during the civil war, under the Jimmy Carter, Ronald Reagan, and George Bush administrations. (Kevin Sullivan and Mary Jordan. "In Central America, Reagan Remains a Polarizing Figure." *Washington Post.* June 10, 2004.)

I related one thing with the other and that same evening when I arrived at my house, I went directly to the box where I kept my most precious objects, and took out the postcard. I looked at it for the last time and tore it to pieces.

While doing this, I told myself, "I've been tricked. The country of the United States is not peaceful like they wanted to appear in this photo. The country of the United States makes war on me and is sending helicopters full of soldiers in order to massacre my people."

For much of my life I thought the same as I did in that moment, until I understood that the evil was not the country of the United States. The evil has been some of the US-backed governments that have come to power and brought war and genocide all over the world.

Genocide is a word that I learned in the clandestine Saturday meetings. I heard it for the first time one night when they were making preparations for a great protest that would reach its climax the next day. I helped make a banner of fabric that said "Ronald Reagan Genocide" in red letters, because the Salvadoran people saw this person as responsible for the blood that ran in great quantities, thanks to the military "aid" that he provided[40]. I know that some who read this do not like to talk about their leaders in this

---

[40] During the presidency of Ronald Reagan (1981-1989), there were extended US military operations in El Salvador (1981), Libya (1981-1986), Sinai (1982), Lebanon and Beirut (1982-1984), Grenada (1983), Honduras (1983-1989), Nicaragua (1986), Bolivia (1986), Iran and Iraq (1987-1988). There were CIA interventions in El Salvador (1979-1992), Afghanistan (1979-1989), Cambodia (1980-1995), Angola (1980's), and Nicaragua (1981-1990). Military aid was given to several other countries. Many Latin American military leaders were trained at the US-sponsored School of the Americas (Ellen C. Collier. "Instances of Use of United States Forces Abroad, 1798-1993." Department of the Navy – Naval History and Heritage Command. http://www.history.navy.mil/wars/foabroad.htm)
(Dr. Zoltan Grossman, "From Wounded Knee to Syria: A Century of US Military Interventions." Evergreen State College. http://academic.evergreen.edu/g/grossmaz/interventions.html)

manner, but it is undeniable that blood was shed through the streets of my country for 12 years, and it was not the result of the people protesting in the streets. Rather, the primary cause was the sending of arms and hundreds of millions of dollars by the government of Ronald Reagan to the army of El Salvador, responsible for the death of eighty thousand Salvadorans that fought because they were hungry.[41] The deaths of poor people and so many others in the history of our planet should embarrass us for allowing psychopaths to occupy roles as important as those held by presidents and governors.

They feel no remorse for carrying out these massive exterminations or for sponsoring crimes as low as the assassination of *Monseñor* Oscar Romero, who was executed by a group of soldiers. They were also responsible for the vile assassination of four American monks from the Maryknoll order[42] and for the countless crimes led by the maniac Salvadoran, who in his wicked life was called Roberto D'abuisson.[43]

This protest that I mentioned earlier, for which I helped to make the banner, resulted in a massive rally that took place in San Salvador. More specifically it occurred in front of the metropolitan cathedral, for the funeral of *Monseñor* Oscar Romero, whose punishment took place one March 24, 1980 while he celebrated mass.[44] The entire population came from

---

[41] The UN Truth Commission reported that more than 75,000 Salvadoran citizens were killed by governmental armed forces during the war (*Report on the Commission on the Truth for El Salvador*. United Nations. http://www.derechos.org/nizkor/salvador/informes/truth.html)

[42] On December 2, 1980 four American women in the Maryknoll order were kidnapped, raped, and killed by the Salvadoran National Guard

[43] Major in the Salvadoran Army, founded the political party ARENA, ordered the torture and death of thousands of civilians during the civil war, and was called a "pathological killer" by the US Ambassador (Richard Severo. "Roberto D'Aubuisson, 48, Far-Rightist in El Salvador." New York Times, February 21, 1992. http://www.nytimes.com/1992/02/21/world/roberto-d-aubuisson-48-far-rightist-in-salvador.html)

miles away to protest such a lamentable death.[45] It was a great activity and there were people from every corner of the country representing different popular movements. Our neighborhood was present and represented by the Union of Slum Inhabitants.

The most numerous and organized were the Farmer Federations, who in reality had the most experience in how to protest and fight. On both sides of Main Street, groups appeared carrying banners and screaming slogans. There were hundreds of people blaming the government for the death of their martyr leader, and without realizing it we were in the center of a real multitude. My father found it appropriate to hold the arms of my two older brothers because of the crowd. My mother held me like a concrete claw.

"This is going to turn out well," commented my father. On top of a car parked beside the cathedral, powerful speakers told the people where they should stand. A beautiful song was played, like background music, speaking of the cardboard houses and the sadness of the people that inhabited them. I took the words of that song to be just for me. I believed that the man singing this song was talking to me, that he knew me, and knew that I searched for my food in the dump. Then another song sounded and this one said that it was not enough to beg; that many things were lacking to achieve peace. I felt like part of the whole thing, because I had known the leader whose death was the reason for this great gathering. In fact, the majority of the banners enlightened his silhouette with the caption, "Oscar Romero lives in the Salvadoran people."

---

[44] Romero was assassinated at the altar after calling on Salvadoran Christian soldiers to stop violating human rights

[45] More than 50,000 people attended Romero's funeral on March 30, 1980 (Latin American / North American Church Concerns of the Kellogg Institute at the University of Notre Dame. "Archbishop Oscar Romero: A Bishop for the New Millenium." http://kellogg.nd.edu/romero/Biography.htm)

Some military vehicles loaded with troops passed by from time to time, always three or four blocks from the concentration. They would stop, and then leave with all speed. The mass of people continued arriving.

Not having done enough already in terms of massacring the people, the government ordered that armed troops be stationed on the tall buildings to watch the people. The canons of the G-3 rifles pointed down from the roofs and from below looked like small streaks in the sky.

No one thought that they would dare to attack, and therefore they succeeded in taking us by surprise. The first shot thundered. After it stopped, a lead storm fell upon the river of people and again the blood of the poor began to run.

The arrogant attack had begun and in an instant I could no longer see my father or my brothers. Everyone was screaming.

Taken by the hand of my mother, I ran where she ran. Everyone's faces lit up like they do when an earthquake or tremor comes upon a city. People ran into one another, hitting each other while searching for refuge or something to protect them from that unceasing storm above. The bullets that did not hit someone's head or body fell in the street, ripping pieces of asphalt.

Some pleaded for help. Others looked to heaven with terrified eyes and screamed prayers. The majority wanted to get in the cathedral but there were already a lot of people there and the main gates had already been closed from inside. My mother and I arrived at a pot that went around a medium-sized tree, and there she threw me on the ground, made me into a ball, and threw herself on top of me. I adjusted my face in a way that allowed me to breathe beneath her weight, and from below the protective shield that was my mother's body, I could see for myself, without anyone having to tell me, how far evil is capable of coming, unchecked by man.

There were many deaths.[46] I saw bodies fall in front of me and on both sides, far away and up close. Of all the human beings I saw die that day, there is one that has stuck with me. In his final instant, he passed in front of us, running disoriented, trying to find refuge behind the tree pot, but it no longer had room to protect him. He then ran to the other side and when he had taken a few steps, knelt upon being discovered and raised his hands absurdly in a sign of surrender, as if this could help him in some way. The bullets continued falling.

I don't know who he was, what he was named, or where he lived. He was a humble boy, about fifteen years old. His face showed hunger like mine. How many nights had he gone to bed, like me, without eating? Had he satisfied his hunger and thirst that day? Had he laughed enough in his short life? I will never know. But I do know that by unintended chance, his eyes saw me and I saw him with mine. Beneath my mother, my eyes did not cease photographing these scenes of hate and unleashed cruelty which I will never forget. I guard them in my memory, like I guard the furtive glance of this unknown boy that looked at me fixedly a second before a bullet fell from above and shattered his face forever.

No one in my family died, but much innocent blood was shed. There were a considerable number of deaths that day. Only half of the 30 people in my neighborhood who attended that "activity" returned home. Some were shot, while others were detained, tortured, and killed later on. Like I said, no one in my family died, but after that we lived in fear. The other half of our lives remained behind, stuck to the asphalt, lying alongside the dead.

---

[46] During the incident, 40 people were killed and hundreds were seriously wounded. 7,000 people fit into the 3,000 capacity cathedral. (Latin American / North American Church Concerns of the Kellogg Institute at the University of Notre Dame. "Archbishop Oscar Romero: A Bishop for the New Millenium." http://kellogg.nd.edu/romero/Biography.htm)

A year passed after that massacre and what came next was more repression. We never had another night free of sounds and voices. Our dreams were filled with lamentations and faraway screams. For that year, things did not change and my parents had another worry. My brother Alberto was now of age to be recruited and this brought all of us more anguish. And so they began to think about abandoning the country, but for this they needed money.

By luck, my father had quit drinking for a long time and his workshop was doing better. He had acquired two new sewing machines and his clients were abundant. My mother had resigned from her work as a servant, and the patron lady, in thanks for the time she had labored, bought her a new television, an electric oven, a radio, and gave some money that my mother kept in a tin piggy bank. Whenever she could or when there were coins left over, she would throw them in the piggy bank, and so the tin jar began to gain weight. One day they took inventory of all the properties and discovered that with the sale of all those things, the saved money, and the sale of the three sewing machines, they could obtain passage for at least three members of our family. They decided that those most endangered should leave first, and those were my father and my two older brothers.

So it was that one morning we all left, on course for the bus station from where they would cross the border. I remember that the three of them climbed onto the bus and it seemed like they did not want to do it. When the bus started to move, the three looked at my mother and I through the window and we all cried. It was the second time in my life that I saw my brother Armando cry; the first was when Hurricane Fifi buried two of his best friends, troublesome like himself, in the mud. My brother Armando, shovel in hand, was one of those that removed the mud without resting in search of the bodies. Armando suffered a lot that day and the whole neighborhood saw him cry inconsolably while he sank the shovel into the mud with desperation in search of his buried friends. Now again he was crying, and the rest of us too, until the bus was lost in sight.

Cathedral Massacre
Police fire on protestors. May 8, 1979.
This attack preceded the one at Archbishop Romero's funeral.

I didn't want to become a bystander
In a city of flames
But even though it happened many wonders ago
A boy remains trapped in this place

Yesterday, today
I walk with my adult motions
Beneath a rainfall of explosive toys

Mother, I'm afraid!
Why does everyone run away
While the boy I'm seeking stays still?

I find myself.
I see him. He sees me.
He tells me, "I am your childhood!"
I tell him, "I am your death!"

And in the darkness of those eyes
We both begin to cry

7

— This is Not a Game —

BEREAVED, SORROWFUL, and without the desire to live, my mother and I returned to the house. There was not even a place to sit down, as everything had already been sold. That whole day, we flung ourselves down to sleep on some rags that for the time being would be our bed. Neither hunger nor the war outside succeeded in waking us up. The following day the same thing happened and I felt like we had died.

It was the third day in which we discovered that life went on and that we should continue to exist. Those days were the most difficult. All my life, my older brothers had defended me, even though there were times when I defended myself. But they were the ones who worried about me and deflected the blows from everyone who wanted to do me harm. That's how it had always been, but no longer. My mother and I had to learn to live without them, and as that was precisely what we needed to do, that's what we did.

One morning, my mother brought me with her to the wholesale market and bought five cartons of eggs. Then we went to the neighborhoods surrounding the city and began to sell them retail, house by house. That gave us enough to live while we waited for news about those who had gone away.

During that time in which we had to sell eggs and plantains and pull heavy packages of merchandise from the market's merchants, I came to understand many things. For example, for the poor man it is sometimes another poor man who humiliates and despises him even more than the rich man. I realized that the poor enter into a competition where they must demonstrate to the rest that they are no longer poor, and sometimes invest all of their income into this competition. A poor man who wants to dress fashionably is nothing more than a reflection of this absurd competition he has against other poor people. Feeling discontent in his own involuntary poverty, the poor man wants to get even with his fellow poor man because it is like seeing himself in a mirror.

I walked with my mother through those neighborhoods, offering our products for resale. We walked through the neighborhood markets that were inhabited mainly, or more accurately, entirely by poor people. Most of them looked at us with contempt, disgust, or malevolent sorrow, as if they wanted to reaffirm with their gestures that they were in a better condition than us, who had to walk beneath the sour sun all day. Sometimes we asked for water to drink and they denied us the water only to give themselves the luxury of telling us no. The poor man in his discontent lashes out against his fellow poor man.

It was also in this season that I understood that discontent does not have to be centered solely against the rich. No, the discontent has to go directly against the inept governments that have governed our countries for years. It is these governments that promote massive migrations to chase after the American dream, which they incentivize with bells and whistles, but it is not our dream. They make it look like our dream in order to rid themselves of the obligation and duty they have to procure conditions worthy of their country's inhabitants so they can live in the country in which they were born. It is these governments that permit those massacres like the one my family and I survived and that are responsible in every case that a country goes to war.

In the end, all of the poor's discontent should be focused towards the governments that are formed by the rich or given power to govern on behalf of the rich. Not all rich people are consciously involved in this process. Some are only victims of what they have been told: how they should behave; what they should and should not do. They have been told how they should look at the poor and see a thief, a criminal, a potential drug addict. But when the truth is revealed to a rich man, and one by one he takes off all the slabs of ancestral stone that have been placed on top of the poor man, he discovers that underneath all those cliché covers, there is a person that can be his best friend. There is a man or woman who has dreams and hopes that one day things will change for the better of everyone.

It was in these long walks of selling with my mother that I started to understand this. I knew that poverty is not a pretext to do nothing or to believe that you deserve a prize for extreme suffering. Poverty is a historical condition that gives no one a free pass to become a criminal, gangster, or eternally resentful. I have become convinced that a healthy coexistence is possible between the rich and poor, without the need for violence to be put forth. While others go about their days crucifying Christ again and again, it is necessary that we give him life with our actions so that each day he may experience rebirth.

Of course, this is not the rosy message of equality sang to the rich and poor, where they are invited to become brothers and take one another by the hand in the chorus of a popular Spanish song. When the song ends, each one returns to his own home and again raises the walls of inequality, those modern towers of Babel that do not help us to communicate better, but on the contrary divide us and distance us from our neighbor, making us indifferent to their hopes and pain.

Before becoming brothers, this message invites us simply to become more humane in all ways possible. Once we succeed in this effort and arrive anew at the depths of our being, we can aspire towards that great privilege of calling everyone in this wide world brothers and sisters. It is about the rich having more solidarity with the poor and together identifying what has cut short our dream. That dream, in the end, is the dream of most people: true and lasting peace.

Sometimes the journey was endless, and every evening before returning home, my mother passed by an office building that had a painting inside featuring all the flags of the world. My mother asked something and the answer was always the same: not yet.

Sometimes we succeeded in selling everything. On, other occasions we returned home with all the goods we started with and my mother would pray with me that the next day things would turn out better. We arrived home in the evening, two hours before the 7pm curfew began. We settled the oven's flames and set the pot above the three bricks, arranged in a triangle, to make coffee. Before night fell, she would go out to buy tortillas, which were sold about two hundred feet from the house.

We didn't have anything left. If we didn't have anything before, now we had even less because we had sold the right to have electricity in order to fund my brothers' and father's trip. Now we lighted the house with a candle that was always blown out by the air currents that filtered through the holes in the old lamina. While we ate a dinner of eggs with tortilla and coffee, I had fun watching my mother's silhouette, projected by the crazy light of the fire. Sometimes the shadow stretched and sometimes it fattened. It kept doing that while I used a piece of tortilla to scrape out a layer of egg that remained in the bottom of the pan.

Without a doubt, my day of walking under the sun and battling with people felt rewarded by this moment with food by the light of a miserable candle. I don't know why, but I felt a special flavor to that food. Sometimes though, we didn't finish eating. In the middle of a bite, the sound of a bullet would shell in the quiet night and a fierce confrontation would erupt.

We put the fire out and the food faded into the background until further notice. The shots thundered on all sides, some stronger than others. The explosion of a bomb was followed by several sudden screams, and the gunshots continued, some close by and others further away. In the corner of the hut, I hugged my mother, tormented by absolute fear. I have never again felt as afraid as I felt on those countless nights.

I closed my eyes in an attack of desperation and tried to use my imagination, like I used to when I observed the postcard of Wisconsin or Massachusetts. My mind once succeeded in devouring the postcard's snowy mountains to mitigate the suffocating heat and thirst, but I couldn't do it anymore. War was real and harder to escape. I wanted to make myself believe that it was only a nightmare that would end when I next opened my eyes. But no, I opened my eyes and the war continued, extracting tears from people, extracting screams that drowned in the sounds of the bullets. Many times, I had to go to sleep hearing this, as if it were a lullaby. The new day would come and we would realize that among the dead were various people we knew: a close friend or a relative.

My mother said that after living through all that, anyone would go crazy, and I believe that in my case this affirmation was proving to be true. I came to confuse dreams and reality. When I was able to sleep, I dreamed of war. I could hear the clear voices of my dead friends, begging me for help. My mother says that I held long, audible conversations with those friends during my sleep, sometimes even laughing or crying. When I woke, the war continued, without any signs of going away.

One day after selling, my mother passed back by the office building and the answer was different this time; they said yes. Thanks to the efforts of my father from outside the country, the United Nations Refugee Agency in Costa Rica had conceded my mother and I refugee status. We had never received better news and from that moment on, like every other time something magical happened in my life, even the air seemed more pleasant. The agglomeration of people pushing each other and talking bad to one another in the streets of San Salvador, the shouts of vendors in the market, and the stalking of thieves, everything was music to my ears after the news.

"Why didn't you tell me that's what we were going there to ask every evening?" I asked my mother.

She hugged me, gave me a kiss on the forehead, and told me, "Because I didn't want to give you illusions. I was afraid that this wouldn't happen." She began to thank God, and did so the whole trip back to the house.

The legal requirements were fulfilled ahead of schedule, and one week later, at 7am on a Tuesday morning, my mother and I waited next to other refugees.[47] They were forming a line in the boarding section of the International Airport of Comalapa.

There weren't many people and the majority were frightened, above all those who could be identified as refugees by their clothes or modest luggage. A UN official accompanied us and told us not to worry, that the worst had already passed. That person was completely right. The worst had already passed, at least for us.

Inside the airplane, which was smaller than I had expected, all the window seats were taken and we were given

---

[47] By 1983, there were 400,000 Salvadorans displaced in the country, 500,000 refugees in the United States, and 200,000 refugees in other Latin American countries. This represented 20% of the country's population. (*Report on the Commission on the Truth for El Salvador*. United Nations. http://www.derechos.org/nizkor/salvador/informes/truth.html)

seats along the aisle. There were three seats to a row, and in our row the window seat was occupied by a man, about thirty years old, who was drinking an iced refreshment out of a clear plastic cup. I sat in the center and stretched my neck in order to see through the window.

The man said he was a Mexican journalist, who for a year-and-a-half had covered and photographed the conflict and was now going happily home. He was very conversational and was reenergized by occasional sips of his iced drink. He showed us his credentials and an album of his best photos of the war. He turned out to be a very friendly type and proved it right away, because when he had asked for another drink, he offered me his seat. I was left emotionally mute because I didn't know that people existed who would give up such important things like their window seat in your first and only airplane flight.

Later, some instructions came in regarding personal luggage, and in a few minutes the airplane began to move very slowly. It turned around onto the runway and finally ran to maximum velocity in a straight line.

It was September 8, 1981. I was about to turn twelve years old and was seated on a commercial airplane next to my mother, fleeing my country of origin. I survived cruel epidemics that killed many children my age. I won the game against hunger, but the war made me lose almost all of my childhood friends, to whom I dedicate all that I write. I knew thirst, the cold, the heat, and the punches and jabs of life. I was born and raised with hunger by my side, as are almost all the children of Latin America. I had left uninjured from the Cathedral massacre, as it is known, and about which a movie and various documentaries were made and shown to the world.[48]

---

[48] The movie *Romero* was released in 1989 and portrays the life and death of Archbishop Oscar Romero.

The Mexican journalist asked for another glass and I thought that he liked that drink a little too much. He turned back towards me and said, "I took many photos of this war. The majority are of the cathedral massacre and I cried a lot while I took them," he said. Then he took a long swallow from his drink and remained in silence. My mother and I also kept perfectly silent and the plane began to elevate.

Through the window, the world seemed distant to me. The houses looked like they were from a drawing. The people down below were just small, moving points from this height. "This must be how the vultures saw me while they flew over the dump where I ate all these years," I thought.

The journalist began to speak again. "The people screamed, pleading for help. I was in the middle of that shameful butchering and it was not pretty. You all are doing well to abandon this country. This war is no child's game," he said, and announced again so that no doubt would remain, "This is not a game." Then, in one swallow he downed half of the contents of the glass. Afterwards, he threw back his head, stretched his legs, and closed his eyes.

"It's true that this is not a child's game," I thought. Through the window, the world seemed fuzzy, almost gray. I looked back to see my mother, with her dark and shiny indigenous hair. Her face seemed satisfied and thankful, like a person who had just been told "your problems end here." She prayed in silence with her eyes closed. Then I saw all the passengers who were seated nearby, their faces drawn in different states of excitement, and finally I threw a glance back at the Mexican journalist.

"It's true. This is not a child's game," I responded to him clearly, without hesitation. But the journalist could not hear me; he was already asleep.

Graduation
Elmer (left) and his father (right) receiving their elementary school diplomas at an adult education center in Costa Rica.

— Afterword —

THERE IS A SUBLIMINAL MESSAGE that permeates the environments of extreme poverty. This message is in the air, in what you eat, and it's transmitted from adult to child, like a fact of life. The message is this: we are poor and we aren't worth a thing.

With this mindset, in which our low worth is inscribed, we leave life in the same way we entered it: confronted by an exclusive society that values you according to your material standing and not for your capacity to love, your sense of justice, or your aptitudes and talents. With this way of thinking, we make ourselves believe that because we aren't worth anything, neither is anything we do worth the trouble.

It may take one's entire life to realize that this message is counterproductive and rebel against it. This will lead us to other battles, which are no less important, and sometimes that battle arises within ourselves. We want to say something, and although we're convinced that we have nothing of value to say, we must proceed in saying it anyway.

In my personal case, I often rebelled against this inherited culture of poverty. Since I was little, I always dedicated myself to the things I liked to do, and therefore, in addition to my labor of finding food, I also found *myself* in that trash dump. It was not easy. Hunger robs strength from reason, but even so, I went about discovering my passion towards literature and painting. In those environments, everything indicated that those activities did not serve any purpose and those who pursued those activities were just as hungry as those who did nothing at all.

What I write, I write under difficult circumstances and without neglecting or interfering with my scheduled duties in the different jobs in which I have labored. Sometimes I have written a chapter during my lunch hour, and while I ate with one hand, I wrote with the other so as not to let the ideas in my head pass by. There were similar occasions where, while the other construction workers slept after an arduous day of labor, I was submerged in my thoughts and surprised when dawn came and I was still writing, when I should have been waking up to start another strenuous workday.

That's when others start to ask, "Why do you do all this? Why do you continue to work after an entire day of grueling labor? Why not rest and have some fun?"

I only have one response for them, "I write to live!" In order to live, we must recognize the need to denounce injustice and rebel, however we can, against the cruelties that torment us from the time we are children, against those things that cannot and should not be forgotten.

I wrote this book to say to myself that we should not wear the word "loser" throughout our lives, but rather the word "PURPOSE," in capital letters. In addition to leaving a tangible footprint of my walk through this world, I want to scream to the four winds that although I was born in extreme poverty, I have a lot to say and it's important, because we the poor are worth as much as everyone else.

Elmer Hernán Rodríguez Campos
November 1, 2014

"Hope"
Painting by Elmer.

— About the Author —

ELMER HERNÁN RODRÍGUEZ CAMPOS was born in San Salvador, capital city of El Salvador, on February 17, 1969. By 1980, war had broken out and he had to leave his country in 1981. He immigrated to Costa Rica as a refugee with the help of the United Nations Refugee Agency and has lived there ever since. He is married to Mileny Vindas Salazar and they have four children: Jordan Vinicio, Andrea Mercedes, Jose Leonel, and Elmer Lautaro.

Since he was little, Elmer has enjoyed drawing, painting, and writing stories and poems. Like most immigrants, he has had to work in various jobs, but has always searched for time to practice the art that he loves. In recent years he has started to paint in public places and sell his artwork as a street vendor, using what he earns to support his family.

Apart from writing and painting, another ongoing project in Elmer's life has been teaching the technicalities of drawing and painting. For 17 years, out of his own initiative and with his own resources, he has taught groups of children in poor communities. They gather every Saturday to draw.

Besides *Under the Sour Sun*, Elmer has written other original works in Spanish, including *Radio Soledad*, a play *Los Helicópteros*, books of poems *La Noche Transeúnte* and *Antes de Morir, Quise Decir Esto*. He is currently finishing a novel entitled *Entre Vos y Yo, La Niebla*, which tackles the issue of domestic violence.

— About the Translator —

TIM HONCHEL was born in Lexington, Kentucky on January 23, 1990 and after moving several times with his parents and two younger siblings, grew up mostly in central Maryland.

After graduating from Asbury University in 2011 and embarking on a variety of transformative experiences in Central America, the inner city, and on farms, Tim began to transition towards a lifestyle in pursuit of social and environmental justice. He now provides strategic planning services to groups and organizations that are moving in a similar direction. He enjoys reading, writing, growing food, and riding a bicycle.

49448545R00064

Made in the USA
Charleston, SC
25 November 2015